Mastering a Healthy Self Image

The Guidebook to Real Happiness and Enormous Success

Darrell Knoch

Published by Imagine Enterprises, LLC
1740 Dell Range Boulevard
Suite H-166
Cheyenne, WY 82009

www.truewealthuniversity.com
Toll Free 800-319-4080

Printed in the United States of America
First Edition: October 2011

Mastering a Healthy Self Image : The Guidebook to Real Happiness and Enormous Success / Darrell Knoch

ISBN 978-0-615-54059-7
Library of Congress Control Number 2011919377

Cover design by Alison Hixson, Chattanooga, TN

Acknowledgments

I am a firm believer that no one is ever truly self-made. Without the help and input from countless people, we would all live a very shallow existence.

There have been so many people—family, friends, employees—who have influenced my life. It is impossible to list everyone who has helped me make my dreams come true. They have enhanced my mindset daily and challenged me to become a better person.

Although these people had a huge impact in my life, it is my mother who gave me my foundation. She fostered my inquisitive spunk that always drove me to ask *why* and *how*, and she gave me her gift of determination. Her words, "You set your own standards in life," and "Never let anyone bring you down to their level," have echoed in my mind throughout my life. I am grateful for all that she taught me.

Also, watching how my brother Fred lived his life taught me the character trait of discipline. This trait has served me well, especially when I needed to accomplish that next goal, but I was tired, or I was having a hard time taking action. I will be forever grateful to Fred for the gift of discipline.

My brother John had a huge impact on my life when he gave me my first set of Zig Ziglar tapes in 1977. This gift brought about a dramatic change in my life and started me down the path of self-education. It triggered the desire to read and listen to tons of educational material and to attend many seminars over the past thirty years. I immersed myself not only in the teachings of Zig Ziglar, but other great speakers as well, such as Tony Robbins, Earl Nightingale, W. Clement Stone, Napoleon Hill, Denis Waitley, Brian Tracy, Les Brown, Tom Peters, and many more.

The teachings of these great speakers had such a profound effect on my life that I cannot thank John enough for that first gift of Zig Ziglar tapes. It was the inspiration that started me on a life-long study of human nature to empower myself and has led me to write this book.

About the Author

Darrell Knoch

Being born into extreme poverty, the youngest of seven children, then having an accident at the age of one that disfigured my face, I grew up with very poor self- esteem and was angry toward the world. Thankfully, I was so determined not to let those things keep me down and define me, that I made the decision early on to do whatever was necessary to overcome the adversities I faced. And I made a commitment to start educating myself, so that when I faced any challenges, I would have the skills to surmount them.

I eventually started several companies that I took national and international. Because of my success with these ventures, I was able to semi-retire at the age of fifty-four.

I have learned a tremendous number of life lessons that I want to share with you through this book. My desire is that you will be able to apply these lessons to your life, so that you can find happiness, and ultimately go out and do great things for yourself and the world.

Table of Contents

Forward

This book is an **absolute** must- have for any person determined to permanently reshape one's self-image. Darrell's words have a touching and empowering way of elevating one's spirit out of the doldrums so many us find ourselves in today. His deep commitment for helping others has led him to his newest quest to help shape and mold humanity for the positive. My only hope is that one would take the chance to engage in the opportunity to forge an unwavering self-confidence! I am extremely grateful Darrell has revealed the path so I could begin the journey.

Dr. Patrick Schinzel, PharmD.

Chapter One

Changing Your World

I believe that we all can have what it takes to make a dramatic difference in the world, for ourselves, as well as for others.

Many of us have had a lifetime of negativity driven into our mind that it alters our self-worth and self-confidence. This negative mindset limits our ability to take the necessary action to empower us for greatness. If we don't live up to our full potential, we will fall short of the true feeling of contentment and the depth of happiness that we can achieve.

Mastering a Healthy Self Image will provide a clear road map which will allow you to start the process of building a healthy self-image and help you discover a deep level of happiness in your life. Once you have learned these techniques, you will be able to enjoy living with a profound appreciation for life and the world around you.

We all have different levels of self-esteem in a variety of areas, depending on how well we perform these specific tasks. There are some things we are *really good at*, while there are other things we are *not so good at*. Our level of performance in each of these areas determines our self-confidence.

The goal of mastering a healthy self-image and finding true happiness is not an overnight process; rather, it is a process that requires commitment and discipline. You'll need to master new behaviors and habits. Not all habit patterns will come naturally, but these new behaviors can be built along the way, as we work to build a healthy self-image.

For most of us, the job of extracting all of the garbage that has been dumped into our minds and bodies takes considerable time. It all starts with the choices that we make each day. Will we continue down the same negative path, or will we feed our mind with positive education, change our attitude, and start down a new road? If you choose a positive path, you will have a more dynamic outlook on your life from that day forward.

Some days will be positive, while other days will test our new mindset, and we will have to work to keep on the new healthy track. No matter where your level of self-esteem is, *it* will improve each day, as *you* work toward improving your life.

Zig Ziglar says that we are all born with the seeds of greatness, so no matter where you have been, and no matter how low you feel, if you look up and go as far as you can see, when you get there, you will be able to see even farther and forge ahead.

Tony Robbins says, "The past does not equal the future." You can and will change, so now it is up to you to choose the path of fulfillment.

The pride you take in yourself has the most value of all.

Over the past thirty-plus years, I have been a student of human nature. I have studied men, women, and children, and the beliefs that have allowed some of them to be much happier and achieve so much more than the average person.

I've learned that a good, healthy self-esteem is the single most important trait in a truly happy, successful person. I am amazed how few people really have strong self-esteem, and I am even more amazed at how fragile most people's self-images really are.

Piers Morgan, of the CNN show *Piers Morgan Tonight*, recently interviewed Jack Welch, the former CEO of General Electric. Piers asked Welch what the single most important trait was for success, and Welch, without hesitation, said it was self-confidence. He added that the next most important traits were clarity and certainty.

I have read thousands of articles and hundreds of research studies and books; and I've listened to countless audio recordings about happiness, self-confidence, and achievement. I have interviewed over 40,000 people, and I have concluded that the foundational traits of happiness and success in every aspect of life are self-esteem and self-confidence. The healthier your self-esteem and the more self-confidence you possess, the more enthusiasm you will have for everything in life.

If you master the qualities of self-esteem and self-confidence, and you have a great deal of enthusiasm, you will be unstoppable. People will gravitate towards you. These people will want to help you achieve your dreams, because people are drawn to those with an excitement and enthusiasm for life.

Every man or woman who has had genuine happiness and has accomplished what we consider greatness, has possessed tremendous self-confidence. When you reach the point where you believe in yourself so strongly that you know you can accomplish anything you put your mind to, your future will be unlimited. Because of their self-confidence, they know that when they start a project they can complete it—and do it well.

If you want to start some excitement in your life, a great question to ask is, "What great things would I dare to dream, if I knew I could not fail?"

What would you do, and how would you think differently, if you absolutely knew you would succeed? What if you had the power to achieve any goal you set? What if you were completely fearless to act on whatever dream or goal you had?

If you developed the quality of unshakable self-confidence, your whole world would transform. If you had a deeper confidence in yourself and your abilities, you would make ambitious plans and set loftier goals, and you would commit to achieving things that you only dream about today.

You would do what you really wanted to do, and you would refuse to conform to the wishes or opinions of anyone else. You would define your life in your own terms and live consistently with exactly what it was that you wanted. You would be greater in every part of your life and career, and you would have greater self-confidence.

You might decide to ask for the promotion or raise you deserve, change jobs or professions, or launch your own successful business. With greater self-confidence, you would be bolder and more imaginative. You would be more creative and willing to experiment with new and different ideas. You would consider unusual and risky alternatives and be willing to commit yourself whole-heartedly to projects, which today, only sit on the backburner of your mind.

If you had unlimited self-confidence, you would be more powerful and persuasive with other people, and you would be welcomed wherever you went. You would speak up and speak clearly in your interactions with others. You would be admired, respected, and sought after by everyone who knew you. Recognition and responsibilities would flow to you because of people's faith in your ability to do whatever it took to do an exceptional job.

Positions of prestige and status would open up for you, and people would bring projects that, at the moment, you could not even imagine. With greater self-confidence, you could deal more effectively with the problems and difficulties that arise in life. You would think continually of solutions, and how you could turn your difficulties into your best advantage. You would laugh at adversities that would dishearten most people, and you would be successful in any endeavor.

You would feel invincible. You would be far more effective in dealing with difficult people and situations, and do so with a higher level of self-confidence. You would be a better negotiator, ask for—and get— superior terms and conditions, and receive a better return on everything that you bought and sold. With an unshakable belief in yourself, nothing would be impossible for you.

More than anything else, you would feel terrific about yourself. And most importantly, you would be happy about every part of your life, knowing that you had the ability to take whatever steps and changes that were necessary to ensure that your life was on track. You would experience a tremendous sense of control over your life, which is a fundamental condition for happiness, well-being, and maximum performance.

You would be the captain of your fate, the master of your soul. You would experience a feeling of complete contentment that comes from the strength and purpose of a positive mental attitude. With an unshakable self-confidence, you would be an exceptional human being.

Thankfully, self-confidence is a mental quality that can be learned. We start learning self-confidence and building self-esteem in early childhood, and because it can be learned, self-confidence can be developed and built over time by using the ideas and practices in this book.

Most people tend to compare themselves to others and sell themselves short. We tend to be plagued with doubts about our abilities and harbor fears about everything imaginable—especially the unknown. We dwell on our weaknesses and limitations and settle for less than what we are capable of achieving.

Instead of pursuing high levels of self-esteem and personal pride, the average person accepts their fate in life and settles for far less than the happiness they deserve, and the greatness that they could accomplish.

A poor self-esteem can often be traced to early childhood and the criticisms we received from our parents, our teachers, our family, and our friends. We see evidence of this in the classic error parents make when they say, what they believe to be harmless comments, "Bad boy" or "Bad girl," or "Can't you do anything right? Suzie is so much better at that then you are."

Another mistake parents make is criticizing themselves in front of their children. One of the most destructive statements I think I have ever heard is, "It would be just my luck for something to go wrong." Most people have been so conditioned with negative self-talk that they say the words without even thinking, or without realizing the consequences of what they have uttered.

Although parents rarely mean for these labels or statements to apply negatively, the child often takes them personally. We often inherit our parents' issues by thinking, "*If my parents have these issues, I must also*."

Being unable to separate the *person* from what he or she has *done* is confusing the *doer* with the *deed*. This is devastating to a child. It is amazing how we continue to pass our negativity on to our children. I am sure my mother was very disappointed in some of the things I did as a child growing up, but she also never missed the chance to tell me she was proud of me for the *good* things I did.

Remember to pass on a positive mindset to your children and others around you every chance you get.

I was in Walmart the other day and happened to pass by

a mother and daughter looking at some shirts. The mother asked the daughter which shirt she should get for "Dad."

I thought it was nice that the mother and daughter were picking out a gift together, but then the mother got very irritated. She begged the daughter to make the decision for her, afraid she would make the wrong choice. I wondered how badly the mother must feel about herself to labor over fairly simple decisions each day and how the mother's mindset was affecting her daughter's self-worth.

Just a few minutes later, I saw one of the Walmart employees moping to the front of the store to start his day as a cashier. He had very little expression on his face. It was apparent that he just didn't want to get to the front of the store to start work. What a shame that someone has such poor self-esteem that he can't relish the opportunity to meet so many new people, and do so with a big smile. Eager to help customers get through the line as quickly as possible, so that they would enjoy the experience of getting to be in his line because it was moving so fast! You can look at what you do as a disgrace, hating every minute of it, or you can look at it as a chance to learn about others and be helpful in their lives! We can—and must—learn to look at things differently if we want to be happy each day.

The good news is that everyone has a certain amount of self-confidence, more in some areas and less in others. By starting from whatever that point is, we can—and must—build a self-esteem and self-confidence that will empower us to do anything we envision, take the necessary action to achieve those goals, and build a level of happiness and contentment that shines like a light from our face! It is possible for everyone!

All around us, there have been men and women with high levels of self-confidence who have gone on to achieve extraordinary things. In studying the lives of these people, we find out that some of them started out with high levels of self-confidence, which they learned from their parents in early childhood.

Most of them, however, started off the same way we start off, and that is with deep down feelings of inferiority and inadequacy. Because of destructive criticism, lack of love, and other mistakes that parents make with us in early childhood, we grow up with diminished feelings of self-esteem, low self-confidence, and a feeling that we are just not good enough in comparison to others.

With low self-confidence, many people work extremely hard on the outside to achieve success, and then, deep down inside, they feel like imposters. This fear of success is really a feeling of unworthiness that we just can't seem to get rid of no matter how much we achieve on the outside.

What people really want is to feel good about themselves. We want to be happy and have a positive sense of well-being. We want peace of mind and contentment. We can only achieve this when we feel confident in our ability to deal effectively with the challenges of life.

The **law of cause and effect** states that if we want high self-confidence, we must only engage in actions and thoughts that build our self-confidence. We must learn what other highly self-confident men and women say and do, and emulate these same traits. Over time, we eventually will get the same results. We will become unstoppable. Tony Robbins calls this "modeling."

In psychology there is the **law of becoming,** which

states that we are in a continual process of becoming, or evolving, in the direction of our dominant thoughts. Your body is also in a state of becoming. While your physical evolution is affected by what you eat and the condition you keep it in with proper exercise, your mental evolution is largely determined by your thoughts.

Whatever you dwell on eventually becomes a part of your mental state, and a part of your attitudes and behaviors. The **law of concentration** claims that anything you think about long enough grows into your reality. The more you envision the person you would like to be, the more these thoughts are cemented in your subconscious and become part of your ongoing evolution.

You are *where* you are and *what* you are partially because of the thoughts that others have put in your mind, and partially because of thoughts you have allowed to preoccupy your mind. Whatever you obssessed about over the years has made you who you are today.

Not only have these thoughts made you into what you are, but you are also continuing with the job of construction with every thought you think. Since this is an unavoidable fact of life, the smartest thing that a person can do is persistently think the thoughts that are consistent with the kind of person he or she would like to become.

One of the most profound discoveries in human history is that **thought is created**. Your thoughts become your realities. You cannot hold one kind of thought and experience a different kind of existence. The development of true happiness and a healthy self-esteem begins with taking responsibility and control of the contents of your conscious mind.

It is important to discipline yourself to think only of the things you want to become, avoiding thoughts of what you don't want. The realization that you are the system that is continuously programming your life will awaken you to a limitless power.

Everything in life is brought about from the inside out. The **law of self-correspondence or self-talk**, which I consider the most important of all the mental laws, states that your outer world will be a mirror image of your inner world. Everything that a person experiences in their outer life corresponds exactly with something that is going on in their inner life.

True happiness and success means living your life in harmony with the laws that govern your being. Even though these laws are invisible, they are like the law of gravity. If we violate them, we will pay the consequences.

Happy people obey the laws of life and live their lives with positive thoughts consistent with those laws. If we want to show self-confidence on the outside, we must have complete integrity on the inside. The real foundation of self-confidence is living life consistently with your inner values and principles while thinking and acting in harmony with your dreams and aspirations.

Men and women with the most rock solid self-confidence are those who are absolutely clear about what is right, good, and worthwhile; and they live their lives accordingly. Everything you say and do is a reflection of your inner truths.

Your whole world can fall apart around you, but as long as you have a healthy self-image and unshakable self-confidence, you will have a deep inner sense of calm that will manifest itself into self-assurance in any situation. You will have many ups and downs in life, but they will not stop you from getting back up and going forward.

My Story

I have filed for Chapter 7 Bankruptcy three times in my life and gone broke a couple more times in between—Walt Disney filed for bankruptcy three times before he created his empire.

No matter what circumstances you've endured, you can pick yourself up and start over. You just have to get back up, dust yourself off, go back after it, and make your life full all over again. You are only a loser if you quit.

My experiences of the highs and lows in my life have given me a deeper insight that I would never trade. I don't care who you are, where you live, what you've done, or what you are doing, I have already walked in your shoes. I can understand your feelings, because I have already felt them and lived them. The story of my life is a story of triumph, but it is not a straight climb to the top.

I was born in Saginaw Michigan, September 20, 1954. We lived in Bay City, Michigan, which is just north of Saginaw. At the time I was born, my dad had a girlfriend in Saginaw, so he dropped my mother off at the indigent care hospital in Saginaw and went to spend the next few days with his girlfriend, while my mother gave birth to me and recovered in the hospital.

In prior and subsequent years, my dad left home many times for one to two years at a time. As I was the youngest of seven children, by the time I was old enough to remember my oldest brothers, they were already leaving home.

One day when I was about a year old, my sister and I were outside playing. I started running toward the road, and my sister, who was ten years older than me, started running after me to stop me from going into the road. As she got close to me, she tripped on the sidewalk and fell on top of me, smashing my face into the sidewalk. This broke my nose and made it very flat and wide.

We were poor and on welfare at the time, so we didn't have the money to take me to a doctor's office or get my nose fixed. We had to just wipe it clean and let it heal. No one had any idea what this would do to my self-image—and later my self-confidence.

As I grew up, my self-image eroded even further as kids ridiculed my nose. The neighborhood kids and my classmates kidded me about having a wide, flat nose throughout my childhood and young adulthood. The ridicule devastated my self-esteem and made me very angry.

We were on welfare most of those years, and welfare

back then was not what it is today. You didn't get food stamps that allowed you to go to the regular store as you do today, and there was no Medicaid. Back then, for the most part, people either received a meager rent allowance or they lived in public housing. We lived in public housing a fair amount of the time, and when we were not living in public housing we were getting rent assistance. All of the housing that we lived in was in very poor repair. It was not unusual for the apartments or houses to have lots of holes in both the walls and the floors. We would put a small sheet of plywood over the holes in the floors, and then put a rug over the plywood so we wouldn't trip. There really wasn't money to paint and have the places look nice, so we just learned to settle for keeping them clean.

We were able to go to the food line with a box and pick up food each week. We would walk through the line and get canned soup, canned ham, boxes of nasty tasting powdered milk, powdered eggs, square logs of cheese, bags of macaroni, and other "delicious" items.

I didn't like the taste of the welfare food very much. My aunts and uncles told me that when I was a young child, I would very proudly say that I didn't care how hard I had to work, I was not going to live like this when I grew up.

Even though she had seven of us to look after, and my dad wasn't around much to help, my mother was a very kind and caring person who loved us all very much, and took care of us as best as she could. I still remember my mother's words, "You can do anything that you want to do, if you are willing to work hard enough to get it." She also said, "Never let anyone bring you down to their level." And, "You set your own standards to live by, and not anyone else's." These three statements—beliefs—, in addition to the way my mother lived her life, were the foundation of the self-image that I started to form.

My mother, all of us, were victims of abuse from my father. He had a temper that unleashed at the slightest incident. I once watched my dad beat my mother until she was lying on the floor with blood coming from her mouth and nose. He kicked her repeatedly as she lay there. It was a horrendous sight that is branded in my mind.

My father would pull off his belt or pull the thin power cord off the latest TV that he was repairing and whip our legs with it until they had large whelps. During the beatings, he would tell us what rotten kids we were for doing whatever it was that got him started.

As Zig Ziglar would say, "Negative, negative, negative."

We were all glad that my father was not around more than he was. As I was growing up, my mother worked as much as she could having seven children, and the more of us who left home, the more she was able to work outside the home. She had a 9th grade education and didn't have a lot of skills to go out to work in the first place. Most of my remembrances were of her working at school in the kitchen lunch program and then cleaning after school.

As I got older, I continued to get teased about my nose. I would get into fights with whoever was kidding me. I would get into trouble often, which didn't help my self-esteem.

I was the little guy in school. I weighed about 125 pounds fully dressed when I was a senior in high school. I was very shy and introverted most of the time. I didn't date much,

I never had the self-confidence to ask girls out. The idea of asking a girl out scared me to death.

When I was eight years old, my mother had me take piano lessons and from that point on, I excelled in music. When I was twelve, I began taking organ lessons. At thirteen, I started trumpet lessons, and began learning to play the drums. By the age of fourteen, I was playing the guitar, and by the time I was a senior in high school, I would tell people that if they gave me a piece of sheet music and an instrument, I could learn that song and play it for them in thirty minutes—no matter what the instrument. I didn't always deliver perfection, but I could play it at least fairly well by the end of the thirty minutes. The saddest part for me was that I was still so shy that when all the girls would scream for me to play and sing, I still didn't have the self-confidence to ask them out. I would have given my right arm to have one of them for a girlfriend, but I couldn't muster the guts to ask.

I played the drums in a local rock band at fourteen, so I played at all the dances that we could line up at all of the junior highs and high schools in my area. I played when I was in college too. Playing music and being in a band was a strong self-confidence builder that began healing a past filled with low self-esteem and poverty.

In my high school years, my dad had gotten old enough that he had come back home to live with us full time. He resigned himself to his local girlfriend and visited her on nights and weekends—but not as much as he had in the past.

With my father around more, we butted heads constantly, because I had become a very scrappy, independent kid and memories of his abuse were seared in my mind.

My father called the police to the house many times to tell me that if I didn't get my act together, they would be sending me to a juvenile home. His threats didn't bother me, and we fought a lot until I was fourteen. That's when he kicked me out for the *first* time—because I played in the band.

I went to live with my best friend, John Medlin, his parents were much more giving than my dad. I stayed with them for about three months, until my mother talked my father into letting me come back home. Once she talked him into it, she convinced me to come back home as well.

Now that I look back on it, I am sure it was a strain on John's family to be paying for my food at the time, so it was a good thing my family and I worked it out. Unfortunately my dad kicked me out again when I was fifteen. This time it was over a girl (at least I was making progress with the girls).

Three of my older brothers had bought a farm about five miles away, so I moved to the farmhouse with them. I worked for my room and board there until I graduated from high school.

This is not a very proud thing for me to admit, but when I graduated from high school I really hadn't had as much good, positive direction as I could have used. I had never read a book from cover to cover in my life. I always read just enough to fake book reports throughout school. But fortunately, one of my brothers, Dan, bought me a book for graduation called *The Beatles Complete*. I was so into music and the Beatles that I immediately read it from cover-to-cover. I realized that I actually *did* like to read—if I had an interest in the subject. At that point I made a life-changing decision and became a reader. This was such a profound experience for me that I must say I will be forever grateful to Dan for that life-changing gift.

As one of the test finals before graduating from high school, two other friends and I wrote a song for one of our classes and played it for the teacher. That was one of the few A's I got during high school. About a year later I went through the process of getting the song copyrighted, because I always like to finish what I start. Accomplishment has always been a great self-image builder for me.

I then decided to go to college. Another event made that possible when my dad faked—in my opinion—a couple of heart attacks. He had managed to get Social Security Disability, and I was able to draw student benefits under his Disability. The Social Security benefits were a great help in my being able to go to college, and I worked part-time as well.

I was not a good student in school. I didn't focus on studying or learning. When I was graduating from the 8th grade, I was given a number of aptitude tests. At the end of the 8th grade, I tested at 3rd grade-6th month spelling level and 4th grade-3rd month reading level. I say this to point out that today I am an avid reader. My vocabulary has skyrocketed from those days, just as yours can, if you make the commitment to study and learn.

By the time I finished college, my older brother Fred was working for the State of Michigan, and he had planned to make a career working for the State. We were very close, and his plan sounded so good to me, that I decided I would follow his footsteps.

Fred had started as an Employment Services Executive.

He had worked his way up to branch manager of one of the larger employment offices and was making what I thought was great money. I applied for the same position he had when he started, and I was hired. I didn't get hired at the first branch I applied with though. I had to apply in several different cities before I was hired. I knew what I wanted, and I was committed to continue interviewing until I got the job. I thought I was on my way to my life's goals.

I believed this career would provide me with a great life, and I felt I was going to be happy with this path. I had every intention of retiring from the State of Michigan after thirty years of service. I would be set for my life.

I then met a wonderful lady and married her. At that point, I knew there wouldn't be anything else I needed. I just had to do my job, be a good husband, and my life would unfold accordingly. I was soon to learn that nothing worked out from that plan.

About two years after I started working for the state, my brother, John, gave me a set of Zig Ziglar tapes called, *See You at The Top: How To Stay Motivated*. This set of tapes so dramatically changed my life that nothing was ever the same again. I will be forever grateful to John for giving me those tapes, because they guided me to great success.

Even though I had been pretty driven to that point, listening to the tapes was like giving my car rocket fuel. I remember to this day, about thirty-five years later, what a negative person I was back then, because when Zig said, "I hope you get a lot out of these tapes, but even more I hope these tapes get a lot out of you," I thought, *He is going to try to sell me something else in the first ten minutes of these tapes.*

Zig claimed that it was very important to listen to the tapes a minimum of sixteen times in order to get the full amount of information, and time after time from then on to continue the motivation. I thought, *There is no way in hell that I am going to listen to these tapes sixteen times, let alone even finish the first time through.*

Again, as Zig would say, "Negative, negative, negative."

Fortunately I *did* keep listening and before I finished with that first sixty-minute tape in a set of six, I knew that I would listen to them sixteen times—and many more—just as Zig had suggested.

Today, I have listened to the original set of tapes so many times that I have worn them out, and I have worn out four more sets since. I have spent thousands of dollars buying other motivational sets of tapes, books, and videos, and I have seen Zig in person at least fifty times over the years.

I participated in as many Tony Robbins events as I could schedule over the next several years, and three times I have walked barefoot over the twelve-feet of red-hot coals. I wouldn't trade anything for all of these life-changing experiences.

I had so much negativity in my head that I needed to immerse myself in all of the good, healthy, positive information I could absorb. I needed this to combat and change all the garbage that had been dumped into me for the first twenty-two years of my life.

I attended many other motivational seminars. I felt like I had a VIP membership to Nightingale-Conant's tape club because I ordered so many sets of tapes, videos, and books. I invested so much money that I think I bought Vic Conant's last house for him. (Not really, it just seemed like it).

I am convinced that these products were transforming me. The speakers' words echoed in my head and exposed me to new, positive thoughts that were worth every penny, because I was never the same.

I have always been a daydreamer. One day I was thinking about all the heat from my wood-burning stove that was escaping up the chimney. Sitting at my kitchen table, I started designing a product that would capture some of the heat and put it back into the living area.

When I was twenty-four years old, I started a company to manufacture the product I had designed. The company eventually grew from my basement into a large manufacturing building in the local industrial park, employing as many as one hundred people and running 24/7 shifts during our peak times. I sold to Menard Cashway Lumber, Home Depot, Lowes, Sears, Ace Hardware, True Value Hardware, among others.

It seemed that the more I learned, the more we grew; the more I learned, the more products I developed. My self-esteem was growing by leaps and bounds, and the more we expanded, the more self-confidence I had to attempt even more.

At one time my products were in almost every major outlet in the country, including every wood stove dealer and distributor in the United States and Canada. I had no knowledge of how to run a large manufacturing company, or how to design products to sell, or how to take them to the market place. I didn't know how to read a financial statement or cost out a product. And I certainly didn't know how to manage people and manufacturing processes. I just *felt* that I could do it.

I had read so many stories about how people made something out of nothing. If they could do it, so could I. Unfortunately, over the first two years, I think I made every mistake possible. I am not sure how we stayed alive with all of those blunders, but I had so much self-confidence that I was sure I could overcome anything.

Some of the mistakes were so devastating that the company barely stayed alive. I could easily have said, "You know, I just am not going to make it. I don't have a clue what it takes to do this like I thought I did." Fortunately I didn't quit, because I had a few more strokes of good luck. I met and hired a retired accountant from the area, and he spent every Wednesday with my staff and me for the next three years, teaching me how to read a financial statement, and how to be an intelligent business owner.

A few months later I met a retired manufacturing engineer who had a Master's Degree in Manufacturing Engineering and had been the plant manager of a very large manufacturing company in town. He spent every Friday with me for the next three years, teaching me all about managing people, manufacturing processes, costing products out, and running and operating a manufacturing facility.

I also hired a management consultant from Detroit. He came up for a few days a month for the next year and a half, and literally stayed at my house for three or four days at a time. We would stay awake half the night talking in more depth about all that I was learning from the accountant and the plant manager.

It was a tremendous learning experience that I could have only dreamed of having—had I even known to ask! Ultimately, I did ask, and what an education I received—all because I wouldn't give up. I realized that I *did* need to learn more, so I did what most people are afraid to do: admit that I needed help. I asked several people in the area if they knew anyone who could help me learn the things I needed to know in order to keep my company alive, which ultimately led to my management dream team!

During this time I attained two patents for some of the products I designed and manufactured. After nine years, I had the opportunity to sell the company to a larger manufacturing company in Chattanooga, Tennessee—and did.

I signed a contract with the buyer agreeing to remain in Chattanooga for ninety days to help transition the customers and teach them the manufacturing processes. After about six weeks of working hard for them, they recognized the value I could provide to them, so they asked me to stay on as National Sales Manager.

I had already fallen in love with Chattanooga, so I agreed and stayed on for another year. Six months into the year my older brother, Dan, who was an expert in Cephalometrics (the scientific measurement of the bones of the cranium and face, used for the evaluation of facial growth and development) and hand tracing x-rays for orthodontists and oral surgeons, started a software development company that was writing software to computerize this process for orthodontists and oral surgeons.

Dan persuaded me to help him get that business off the ground and launching it in the market place. By the end of the year, I decided to get involved and help my brother grow that company.

It was a start-up company just like my manufacturing company, so I knew it would be a lot of hard work. I felt ready for a new challenge and jumped headfirst into Dan's new business.

Over the next six years, we grew his company—with very little money—to the point that we had a distribution network in thirty countries. I was on a plane and on the road so much that I didn't know what my home looked like.

The travel was a lot of fun, and I learned a great deal about what we were selling, as well as how to grow a business internationally. I met with orthodontists, oral surgeons, general dentists, and plastic surgeons all over the world. I became an expert in the field of Cephalometrics and computer video imaging for these medical and dental specialties.

Brian Tracy always said that if you read for one hour a day for one year that you will become an expert in a field, and if you read for one hour a day for five years that you will have enough knowledge to be considered an international expert. I read tons of articles, and studied with some of world's foremost experts in these fields for over six years, soaking up every piece of information I could.

After six years of being on the road, I was worn out and decided I needed a break, so I left the company and rested for a couple of weeks. I was still so driven I could not just sit and do nothing, so I started looking through the "Help Wanted" section in the paper.

I saw an ad for a job as a sales representative for WorldCom, formerly LDDS. We had switched our company's long distance provider to LDDS about a year earlier—which cut our bill in half, so this seemed to be an intriguing opportunity. This sounded like a great job, because it was all local selling, which meant it would allow me the chance to meet local friends and business owners, and also have more stability and involvement in my community.

I thought, *Wow, what a worthwhile opportunity!* I could save a number of businesses a lot of money. What I didn't know was that everybody and their brother were in this business, and it was a very competitive, cut-throat industry.

After about a month, I began to doubt myself wondered if I had made a big mistake and needed to look for something else to do. I could have quit—and I certainly thought about it—but I didn't.

I ended up landing a pretty large customer not long after that, which gave me the confidence to keep going. By the end of the year, I had landed the largest customer in the state of Tennessee and continued on with similar results.

In 1997, I won the Sales Person of the Year award for the Mid-Atlantic region. I also won the President's Club award all five years I was with WorldCom, and I was lucky enough to be awarded 10,000 shares of stock options over that period of time.

I discovered that telecommunications was a very technical business, so I had to learn a lot to sell this much service, since I had no knowledge of the industry at the onset. I repeated the same method that worked before; I read everything about all the products I would be selling.

I had a good Sales Manager who spent time with me and taught me the things I needed to know. I also had the good fortune of befriending a few telephone technicians and business owners who were extremely knowledgeable. They were providing their services to some of my customers, and over the next few years I soaked up as much knowledge as I could from these experts. I am forever grateful to all of these people who were so instrumental in teaching me all the things that helped me be so successful.

The last venture that I embarked on, before semi-retiring and writing this book, was in the real estate and real estate investing business. One Saturday, during the time I was working at WorldCom, I was at the health club walking on the treadmill and watching a TV that was attached to the equipment. As I was flipping through the channels, I came across a Carleton Sheets infomercial. I admit, he got me excited about the real estate business. I owned the course, he was offering, but it had been in my closet for the last two years. It was time to dust it off and get started.

That afternoon, I took it out of the closet, and wrote out a goal to have read, watched, and listened to all of the materials in the course at least once by June 30, 2000. Throughout the process of studying all the materials, I started formulating a plan to buy my first property by July 1, 2000, and to buy two more single-family homes and one multi-family property by the end of my first full year working in this business.

I had a strategy planned out that by the end of ten years, I would own fifty properties. Then I could semi-retire and just manage those properties. I have always written out a detailed plan of what I wanted to accomplish, and I try to write down how I think I will go about making these things happen.

Things don't always go as you plan, and experience has taught me that if I ever fail to have some form of a plan, I rarely get very far before I quit. But if I have a plan, I almost always accomplish more than I originally set out to do. With this in mind, I met with a realtor that I knew from a networking group and asked him if he would help me find some of my properties. I showed him my plan and talked about what I would accomplish. By the end of lunch, he told me that he thought my plan was so detailed and well-thought out that he wanted to join me as a partner. We agreed to start this project as partners and go for it.

Just as an example of how things don't always go as planned, I had written down that I would buy my first house by July 1, 2000; but as it turned out, we didn't end up buying that first house until July 14th, 2000. Over the next year, we put our heads down, dug in and continued working my plan, looking for properties, putting our financing together, and doing all the other things that are necessary to run and build a successful real estate business. I continued to study real estate and learn about all aspects of the business. By the end of the year, we had bought eleven properties.

On one end, things didn't go as planned, and I didn't make my first goal; but on the other end, we went way beyond—and over—the plan. The key was that I didn't let the fact that I didn't make my first goal stop me from pursuing my dream. Also, I was so focused on achieving my goal that I wasn't focusing on the money. I focused on enjoying the process of achieving my goals, and over the next ten years we re-evaluated and re-wrote our plans every year. We then continued down the path of making these plans work.

Over that decade we bought, built, rehabbed, and sold over six hundred properties. This included purchasing and building single-family homes, developing subdivisions, and building and owning mini-warehouse complexes and several office buildings. We also owned the local Re/Max franchise, and had part ownership in a local mortgage company, two title companies, an insurance agency, and several other businesses in and around the Chattanooga area.

We also started and ran a seminar company that taught real estate investing to people all over the United States. Not only was I the managing partner for all of the companies, but I also criss-crossed the country speaking to real estate investment clubs and promoting our real estate investment seminar. We built a very successful business through a lot of planning, relationship building, and good old-fashioned hard work.

Over the years, whenever I spoke at a Small Business Development seminar or some other function, people would ask me what the magic was that enabled me to be so successful. I would respond, "There is no magic. I just go out and do it." Then one day it hit me. I did have the magic that alluded them, and that magic was self-esteem, self-confidence, passion, discipline, and a goal. These are the ingredients that allowed me to have so much success over the years, and they are ingredients that you can acquire and nurture—if you decide to.

It is truly amazing what you can accomplish when the image you have of yourself changes and you begin to see yourself in the proper light. I continued to listen to as many sets of audio-tapes as I could over the years and continued to feed my mind with positive, self-building information each day. In doing so, I continued to grow as a person.

Two insights of the "wisdom of the ages" are: *you are*

going to perform exactly the way that you see yourself, and *you will not perform beyond that which you think you are capable of doing.* The reason that more people don't accomplish more is that most people don't have the self-confidence and self-esteem that they should, and they don't believe they deserve success; they don't believe they are entitled to it.

If you don't think you deserve success, history—and my experience—show that most people just don't try. But if you teach yourself to dream, you will start seeing yourself as having whatever it is that your mind can create.

I share my life story in such detail because history shows that if you can see that someone else, in similar circumstances, can pull themselves up from very little and make great things happen, you can too.

I believe that the greatest gift you can give to anyone is to not give them part of what you have, but rather to teach that individual how to use the gifts they already possess and how to cultivate and nurture the ones they need in order to accomplish their dreams.

You get the best out of others when you give the best of yourself. Many people in life have gotten a lot further than they thought they *would* because someone else thought that they *could*.

I have had a number of friends and acquaintances that I have watched grow and develop from meager beginnings to stunning heights. I have also watched many that have had great talents stumble and fall and never get back up. They have literally wasted their life instead of accomplishing what they could have and contributing to the world.

Zig Ziglar believed we are all morally obligated to earn as much money as we honestly can, because that is the best way that we can help others. There are so many worthy causes out there that no matter what your specific interest is with regard to helping others, it seems there is always someone who shares your interest in that same problem. If you give to those causes, it will grow your self-esteem by leaps and bounds.

I have had the good fortune to help many causes and countless people over the years, and I can tell you that all of these experiences have enriched my life and provided me with great feelings of self-worth.

The Power of Positive Believing

Self-confidence and self-esteem go hand in hand with happiness. The more self-confidence you have, the more things you will attempt, and by the law of averages, the more things you are likely to achieve. The more confidence you have, the less you will be affected by temporary setbacks and disappointments. The more confidence you have, the more likely it is that you will have a long, exciting life, full of rich rewards and satisfaction. Helping you achieve these goals is the reason I wrote this book.

The starting point of self-confidence is to recognize your tremendous strengths and abilities, as well as great character, which will allow you to accomplish anything you want.

You are extraordinary and unique. The odds of there being anyone who has the same combination of talents, skills, and abilities that you own are astronomical. There are wonderful things that you can accomplish that no one knows—not even you.

But what we do know is that virtually everything worthwhile that you achieve will come from your ability to identify your greatest strengths, and then capitalize on them accordingly. Each person has one or more areas of excellence that, properly executed, would enable him or her to accomplish anything.

Those who are achieving the most in every field are invariably those who have pin-pointed their greatest strengths, and who have educated themselves on what they want to do. They then work continuously on those goals until they achieve them.

Education is so readily available today, more than ever before, with the Internet. Every library; thousands of McDonalds; Starbucks, and every other coffee shop, not to mention shopping malls, restaurants, book stores, and airports have Wi-Fi available for you to spend as much time as you could possibly want reading and educating yourself on any topic imaginable.

It is mind-boggling how many Wi-Fi hot spots have become available throughout the world. You can purchase a Wi-Fi netbook or tablet for roughly $250, and you can easily carry it to anyone of the millions of hot spots, even if you don't have your own Internet access. With the Internet and your imagination, it is unlimited as to what you can dream and achieve.

I have always said that the thing you are interested in and can get excited about is what you should be doing. In one study of millionaires, they found that those who were extremely interested in what they were doing were the ones who built fortunes. When they studied the attitudes and decisions of those same people, they found that every millionaire had one thing in common: they had chosen a field they were passionate about. They pursued a vocation that fascinated them and they threw their whole heart and soul into becoming the very best in their field. They had never stopped learning, growing, and continually improving as they went forward.

The conclusions of the study were that success, wealth, and happiness seemed to occur when a person was completely preoccupied with doing what they loved. Most of the wealthy people in this study never set out to make a lot of money. Instead, they set out to find a field they really enjoyed, then they devoted themselves to it. The money came as an afterthought. The reason I have been as successful as I have at so many things, is that I always cared more about my customer than I cared about the money.

To enjoy high levels of self-confidence and self-esteem, you must be working at the edges of your comfort. You must be stretching your capabilities continually. You must have a feeling that you are growing daily with the challenges that your work demands. Without that feeling of challenge or growth, you will experience discontent, and this discontent can serve as a gauge that keeps you grounded. Discontent and dissatisfaction can bring about constructive change that puts you back on track and starts you growing again.

I have spoken about how important values are to your self-confidence. Men and women with clear values and goals who are living their lives with their highest aspirations are those who have the deepest sense of self-confidence and well-being.

The most important values you can have are honesty and

integrity. Honesty and integrity are the core values that are the foundation of all the others. Honesty and integrity have nothing to do with paying your bills and credit cards when they are due. *Honesty is what you do in the dark*, as Zig Ziglar would say. It is the way that you deal with yourself. It is the way that you look at things in a manner wherein you yourself know that what you are doing or saying is the right thing.

If you are going to get the things you want, you have to build character. Having honesty and integrity means that you will never compromise what you believe is right. It means looking at yourself honestly, warts and all. Your feelings of integrity will guide your choices and behavior, they are the most accurate guides to doing what you already know is right.

Fear, not ignorance, is the single greatest enemy to self-confidence and contentment. People are afraid to do what their heart yearns for. But when you build yourself up and gradually overcome those fears, your whole world opens up for you.

Your self-confidence will rise so high that limitations will disappear and you will discover that you *can* follow through on what you attempt, and your commitment will be much greater.

To follow your heart, you don't need to make dramatic changes in your life or relationships. What you *do* need to do is to see yourself clearly and gather the courage to focus on your strengths and your greatest potential. I promise you, when you do this, you will feel the confidence build, and you will know that you have made some of the best decisions of your life.

Although we all have great strengths, no discussion of this kind would be complete if we didn't have the discussion of weaknesses. No matter how strong we are, we all have weaknesses. In fact, people have far more weaknesses than strengths. You may be strong in some areas, but weak in other areas. Weaknesses are an unavoidable and inevitable fact of life. The challenge with human weakness is that unsuccessful and unhappy people have a tendency to focus on them. They become preoccupied with their weaknesses and think about their inabilities far too much of the time. They lose sight of their strengths, and that those strengths can be developed to grow even stronger. They don't have the education or the vision to know that these strengths can and will bring them everything that they want. Instead, they dwell on their areas of weakness.

As discussed earlier, the law of concentration has the greatest impact on the person you become. Whatever you focus on grows and develops, whether good or bad. Great achievers are those who focus on their strengths and abilities. People who focus on their weaknesses and inabilities rarely go out and accomplish much. So, to develop and maintain high levels of self-confidence, you must consciously choose to focus on your strengths as much as possible. An excellent question you can ask yourself is, *What can I do that will make an extraordinary difference in my life?* Success comes from staying with a particular project until you succeed. Every great achievement is preceded by an extended period of dedicated, concentrated effort.

The importance of self-assessment is a critical part of success. There is very little to be gained by "digging," if you are digging in the wrong place. You have to have a clearly defined plan if you are going to do great things with your life.

There's an old adage: "If you fail to plan, then you are planning to fail." It is not always clear to everyone how to define *what* and *how* your life is going to be led, but I urge you to sit down and write out a plan for obtaining your goals. Do the best that you can and reassess as you go. You'll find guidelines for doing this in upcoming chapters.

Just by contemplating a structured plan puts you into the top ten percent of the world. Think about that for a minute.

Here are some helpful thoughts; *Every weakness can be looked at as a muscle that needs to be strengthened.* For example, I used to work with an extremely aggressive personality who found himself in a management position. As a manager, his extreme aggressiveness made him the type of person no one wanted to cooperate or work with. What we had forgotten was that his major skills were in selling. His aggressiveness was a strength when it came to selling, but a weakness when put into a management position, because his brash strength was not being used properly. Many of the so-called weaknesses you have might be strengths that you are using in the wrong place, for the wrong purposes.

One of the reasons that I have written this book is to give you the tools for self-evaluation, so that you can redesign your mindset and overcome the roadblocks that hold you back. These tools will allow you to cultivate your creativity and enthusiasm and uncover the passion and desire to drive you further in your quests.

Do you realize that you are the only person in existence who will ever be able to use your ability? If you don't use it, it is going to be wasted and gone forever.

Earl Nightingale stated, "*You are where you are because that is where you want to be.*" I have pondered that statement many times and have come to realize that if we have been given the wrong directions in life, then we are where we are because we followed directions that took us down that path. If we make a new set of directions for life, we can create our own roadmap based on better directions.

If you are in Kansas and you want to go to Los Angeles, but someone gives you the directions to San Francisco and you follow those directions, you will be lost. If someone that has been unhappy and unsuccessful most of their life gives you the guidelines on how to be happy and successful, you probably will never be happy and successful. However, if you get those guidelines from someone who is extremely successful, then you are much more likely to end up happy, successful.

Scientists have done extensive research on the implications of how the brain functions. Although we have much to learn in understanding the mechanisms in the brain and the central nervous system, we are aware of the inexplicable relationship between psyche and soma—the mind and body. There is a definite reaction in the body as a result of the concerns of the mind.

What the mind harbors, the body manifests in some way. When our fears and worries turn into anxiety, we suffer distress. This distress activates the endocrine system in our bodies, causing the production of hormones and antibodies to change. Our natural immune system is stunted and our resistance levels decrease. We become more vulnerable to outside bacteria and viruses and other environmental hazards.

In her proactive book, *The Aquarian Conspiracy*, Marilyn Ferguson describes the brain's influence on every function of the body, such as heart-rate, immune response, hormones, and so forth. She says that an alarm network links its mechanisms and has a kind of dark genius, organizing disorders appropriate to our most exotic imaginings. I have always maintained that ulcers are not what you eat, they are what is eating you. There have been cases where hay fever and asthma attacks have literally been brought on by patients simply as a result of them seeing pictures of goldenrod or from holding a plastic rose.

Ferguson states that when we describe how we feel, we may be forecasting our own future. If, for example, we say we feel "picked on," or that someone gives us a "pain in the neck," we may literally end up with acne or neck spasms. Strong emotions and loneliness associated with what we call a "broken heart" can actually lead to heart failure.

There is also an apparent link between bottled up emotions and the growth of tumors or other cancers. A splitting headache may be precipitated by someone being pulled in opposite directions, and a rigid personality has been identified as a factor in some cases of arthritis. But when we are happy and excited about life, our body behaves in a much more positive way. **You become, and you are, what you believe.**

What is your daily lifestyle, routine, and conversation with yourself as far as your health and happiness are concerned?

Following is a news story I read years ago:

It was Saturday, November 1, 1980, and Arnold Lemerand was taking a stroll. He heard some children screaming and hurried to where they were playing near a construction site. A massive cast iron pipe had become dislodged and rolled out on to the children, pinning a five year old underneath it.

The boy's head was being forced into the dirt directly under the huge pipe and suffocation appeared to be imminent. Arnold looked around, but there was no one around to help him in the rescue. He did the only thing he could: he reached down and lifted the 1800-pound, cast iron pipe off the boy's head. After the incident, Arnold's grown sons tried to move the pipe, but they couldn't even budge it an inch. In an interview with The Associated Press, Arnold, who was 56 at the time, said that he had suffered a major heart attack six years before the incident.

"I try to avoid heavy lifting," he said, smiling, with the young boy's arm around his neck.

We hear about such miraculous power surges every so often. We hear of mothers lifting cars and firemen who have made impossible rescues in burning buildings. Those kinds of stories used to sound rather questionable to me, so I was always one to check their validity. But in recent years, I have become a believer in the power of positive believing and what it can do.

At one of the seminars I attended, the presenters described the research of Dr. Avram Goldstein, Professor Emeritus of Pharmacology at Stanford University. Dr. Goldstein and his associates had suspected the existence of substances in our brains that are similar to morphine and heroin.

In 1971, they located receptor areas in the brain that act as "locks" which only these substances would fit, like keys. Along with other researchers who were working independently in their own labs, Goldstein discovered that our brains contained these keys in the form of natural hormones. Several have been identified, including enkephalins, endorphins, beta-endorphins, and dynorphins. All of these hormones serve as natural pain relievers, many times more powerful than morphine. Beta-endorphin, for example, is fifty times more powerful than morphine, and dynorphin is a hundred times more potent than morphine.

Scientists already knew that hormones played an important role in regulating certain processes. For instance, adrenaline is the hormone that enables us to fight or flee in the face of danger, calling for peak physical performance. Insulin regulates the sugar levels in our blood. Now these later discoveries are showing us that morphine-like hormones are being produced in our own bodies to block pain and give us a natural high.

In 1978, a University of California research team worked with a group of volunteers who had just had their wisdom teeth extracted. Some of the participants received morphine to combat their pain, while others received a placebo, which they believed to be morphine. By measuring the difference in responses to the "powerless" placebo and the drug, the drug's effect was tested.

Many of the placebo recipients said they had dramatic relief from their pain; however, when a drug was given to them that blocked the effects of the endorphin, the pain returned almost immediately. The test confirms something that is very important for you and me to remember and understand.

When a placebo is given and the individual believes that he or she is getting relief, the brain releases chemicals to substantiate the belief. In many respects, the placebo effect is an act of faith. If our thoughts can cause our brain to release adrenaline from the adrenal glands to help a 56 year-old heart patient lift an 1800 pound cast iron pipe, and if our thoughts can produce natural pain relievers called endorphins that are fifty to a hundred times more powerful than morphine, is it not possible for us to use this power of positive believing in our everyday life, with the only side effect being happiness? You bet it is.

As you start to use the power of this mindset, people around you will notice, and they will ask you why you are so pumped, or why you always have a smile on your face. Won't that be nice to hear?

You know, optimism is an incurable condition in a person that has the power of positive believing. A real optimist will believe that most disease, distress, and dysfunction can be cured. Optimists are also prevention-oriented. Their thoughts and activities are focused on wellness, health, and success.

If you haven't read *The Anatomy of an Illness*, a best-selling book published in 1981, I highly recommend it. The author, Dr. Norman Cousins, was hospitalized in 1964 with an extremely rare, crippling disease. When conventional medicine failed to improve his condition, and he was diagnosed as incurable, Cousins checked out of the hospital.

Being aware of the harmful effects that negative emotions can have on the human body, Cousins reasoned that the reverse must also be true. He decided to dwell on becoming well again. He borrowed a movie projector and prescribed his own treatment plan consisting of Marx Brothers movies and old

Candid Camera reruns.

He studied all aspects of his disease, and with the help of his physician, learned what would have to take place in his body to make it well again. In his book, he recounts that he made the discovery that ten minutes of hard belly laughter would give him at least two hours of pain-free sleep. What had seemed to be a progressive, debilitating, and fatal cellular disease was reversed, and in time, Cousins completely recovered.

After his personal account of his victory appeared in the *New England Journal of Medicine*, he received more than 3000 letters from appreciative physicians throughout the world. Medical schools have included his article in their instructional materials, and in 1978, Norman Cousins joined the faculty of the UCLA School of Medicine. Norman Cousins learned the power of positive believing and used it to cure himself. You too can learn to use it to empower your life for whatever great things you want to achieve.

I have a very close friend in Cleveland, Tennessee, named Bob Pritchard. Bob is a high school math teacher. I have known him for several years. I first met Bob when he and his wife, Amanda, came to one of our one-day real estate investment seminars, and subsequently came to our four-day boot camp to get fully immersed in the business.

Bob started off with a bang, buying and selling several houses, and making enough money in just a little over a year to pay off every debt he had—and build a sizeable savings account. I was sure Bob was going to continue buying, fixing, and selling houses for a long time to come. I couldn't have been prouder of one of my students.

He lived close enough that we stayed in pretty close contact. Bob even became a licensee for one of my companies. About two years ago, I was having dinner with Bob, and he told me that he had lost a lot of weight. He said that he had been to his doctor a few times. The doctor told Bob that he thought he had a rare disease and probably had only a few to several months to live.

I was stunned and saddened. Bob and I talked about his life-threatening illness for some time and continued discussing his medical situation over the next few months. After some time, he told me that the doctors had changed their minds regarding his diagnosis several times, but he still didn't seem to be getting any better and was afraid for his life.

I told him that I wanted him to listen to several CD sets, such as those by Zig Ziglar, Tony Robbins, Denis Waitley, Brian Tracy, and Norman Cousins, because I believed that whatever illness he had, he needed to use his mind to cure himself. He wasn't getting a cure from anywhere else, and I felt he needed to gain control.

Having this illness was so intense and overwhelming to Bob that he was open to taking a chance and doing something that most of his family felt was nonsense. He bought the CDs from Nightingale-Conant as I suggested and started listening to them.

Bob told me that he listened to the CDs on his daily commute, as well as during his exercise routine, which meant that he was spending at least two to three hours a day feeding his mind. Within a month, Bob was already doing much better. Within a few more months, he told me that his wife had noticed a dramatic difference in his health. Even his children told him that they could see the difference in him.

During the illness, Bob suffered from severe chest pains and shortness of breath to the point that he was sure he was going to die on several occasions. He had also lost almost forty pounds—and was fairly slim prior to the illness.

As he continued listening to the CDs, he regained a good share of the weight he lost, and his shortness of breath and chest pains lessened greatly. Bob concluded that, to the best of his knowledge, his physical symptoms were brought on by incredibly severe anxiety, to the point that it was almost killing him. As he started listening to all the information on the tapes about having a healthy self-image and taking control of his mind, the anxiety and its physical effects all but went away.

He came to visit me in Arizona earlier this year, and we climbed Camelback Mountain together. He seemed to be as healthy as he could be. Not only was he in good physical health, but he also had a much different outlook on life. He told me that he could see the impact that taking control of the negativity within his mind was having on his children. Your mind controls your body, and Bob took the massive action to change his mindset. Not only did this save his life, but it had an enormous, positive effect on his family members and others around him. That really is the power of positive believing!

I like myself, I love my life, I am excited, I am happy, I am healthy, and I add brightness to the life of everyone I meet.

Chapter Four

Building an Attitude Foundation

The starting point of developing high levels of self-confidence, and becoming an exceptional person, is to think through and decide upon your values.

It is important to decide what it is that you believe in and what you stand for, and even more, what you will *not* stand for. What would you pay for, sweat for, and maybe even die for?

Do you value your family, your health, your work? Do you value principles such as freedom, liberty, and compassion for those less fortunate? Do you have reverence for life? Do you believe in honesty, truth, sincerity, hard work, and success? Whatever your values are, think them through, and write them down.

A useful exercise is to think of the men and women, living and deceased, whom you most admire. What qualities in these people do you consider to be most important? What do you look for in your friends and associates when you are trying to decide whether or not to become deeply involved with them? What do you think are the fundamental qualities or values that underlie business and personal relationships?

The act of selecting your values is also the act of clearly stating to yourself, and sometimes to others, exactly how you will live from this moment forward. Once you have selected a value and declared it to be one of your principles, you are saying that this is something about which you will never compromise. Your level of adherence to the values you have selected is the real measure of your quality as a human being.

Unshakable self-confidence comes from an unshakable commitment to your values. When deep down inside you know you will not violate your highest principles, you develop a deep sense of personal power that enables you to deal confidently and honestly in almost any situation.

No one is perfect. We all make mistakes, and we all have issues that get in the way of us living at our highest level. The exercise of writing down your goals will be a powerful influence on your personal evolution, and it will catapult you forward, touching everything you do.

The principle of integrity is a law of the universe. Whenever you compromise your integrity, there seems to be a great force that will not allow you to get away with it. Integrity is an absolute requirement for living an honorable life.

A compromised integrity, failing in being consistent with your values, brings about a "punishment that fits the crime." Whether it is in business, politics, or personal life, it will inevitably create a high level of stress, unhappiness, and inner turmoil. The need for absolute integrity requires that you live in the truth with all people and under all circumstances. Living in truth means that you never live a lie. It means that you always do and say what you know to be right and true no matter what the short-term cost.

You will face life and your relationships and circumstances exactly as they are, not as you wish them to be. Living in truth, you never stay in a situation that makes you unhappy, or in one that for any reason feels wrong for you. Living in truth means that you set peace of mind as your highest goal and your core-organizing principle. You select all the other goals to be consistent with it. You never compromise your peace of mind for anyone or anything else.

You do and say only the things that feel perfectly right for you. You accept your thoughts and feelings completely, whatever they are, and you systematically change each part of your life that is not giving you peace of mind. Only in this way can you enjoy the high levels of self-confidence that are experienced by the successful individual. Only in this way can you feel really terrific and be successful in all of your relationships.

Living consistent with your values is the key to happiness, harmony, and well-being. Your true values are always expressed in your actions—in what you do. Whenever you are under stress and pulled in two directions at once, with opposing demands or responsibilities, your true values show through.

Your actions will tell you which value is most important to you. It is not what you say, or hope, or wish, but only what you do that counts. Your choices are telling you who you really are. If a person says that their family comes first, and that person has to choose between working late or going to a child's soccer game, if he or she chooses the child's needs over the boss's requirements, then they are living consistent with their highest values.

Everyone has had the experience of walking away from a job or relationship, even though considerable sacrifice was involved, because it was the right thing to do. Everyone remembers how great they felt as a result. One of the finest natural highs you can experience is to choose a higher value and act on that value, no matter what the cost. It will always turn out to be the right thing to do.

You can develop a superb set of values by acting as though you *already* have those values. The more you act the part, especially when you demonstrate these qualities under stress when you feel like doing or saying something else, the more rapidly these qualities become a more permanent part of your mental make-up.

In mental development, there is a principle called **resistance**. In weightlifting, muscles are developed by the slow lifting of heavy weights. The heavier the weight and the greater the resistance, the more blood runs into the capillaries and the bigger the muscles become. The same principle holds true when developing mental muscles, especially the mental muscle of self-confidence.

When you discipline yourself to do or say the right thing, especially under stress, you create resistance to natural tendencies. This resistance generates friction. This is the same kind of heat that when applied to a crucible of chemicals, will cause the chemicals to crystallize and take on a new form.

You create friction by resisting your natural tendencies when you choose to do what you know is right and consistent with your highest values, especially when it is difficult. The mental heat causes your values to crystallize at a higher level and become a permanent part of your character.

Every time you do this, you will feel positive, and excited about yourself. Your behavior will further crystallize and become a more permanent part of the exceptional human being that you are in the process of becoming.

Denis Waitley says that he used to think the "seeds of greatness" were special genes or inborn talents. However, after twenty years of research and fifty years of first-hand knowledge, he learned that the seeds of greatness were not dependent on the gift at birth: the inherited bank account, intellect, skin-deep beauty, color, or status. The seeds of greatness are attitudes and beliefs.

We must feel love inside ourselves before we can give it to others. Simple, isn't it? If there is no deep, internalized feeling of value inside of us, then we have nothing to share with others. Oh sure, we can need or be dependent upon people. We can look for security in our relationships, indulge them, flatter them, and attempt to buy them. But we cannot truly share or give love to anyone else until we learn to love ourselves.

If fear prevents us from being loved and expressing love, how do we let go of it? What do we tell our subconscious that harbors our feelings toward others and ourselves? I believe the way to conquer fear is to understand its roots, soften the earth around it with enlightenment, and finally, pull out the fear.

Fear is expressed in a variety of forms. First there is the **fear of rejection,** which is being made a fool of or a failure in the sight or presence of others. Second, is the **fear of change,** which is charting unknown waters—being first, or breaking tradition and sacrificing external security. Third, is the **fear of success**, which is an expression of guilt associated with our natural desire for self-gratification.

As children reach school age, they get negative messages from parents and peers at every turn. Even in college and our professional life, it isn't much different. Individuals who are subjected to environments full of put-downs and criticism often become critical adults with inadequate self-esteem.

The fear of rejection becomes the fear of change; consequently, we seek security in positions where we go *with the system* rather than *rock the boat.* The fear of change translates into the **fear of success**. The fear of success, in my estimation, is just about as strong as the fear of rejection.

The fear of success syndrome, which paralyzes the majority of our society today, is really the fear of trying. Its manifestations are rationalization and procrastination. I hear it in conversation every day when people say, "I cannot imagine myself successful. I can see it for you, but not for me."

Most individuals don't realize that common people have become uncommonly productive by believing in their own worth. They have observed individuals who have overcome enormous handicaps and roadblocks to become great, yet they find it hard to believe the same success can come to them. They resign themselves to mediocrity and even failure, wishing away their lives. They develop a habit of looking back at past problems, which I refer to as **failure reinforcement**. They imagine similar bad performances in the future, which I call **failure forecasting**. They are controlled by rejection and acceptance standards set by others and often set their sights unrealistically high, without a true belief in the validity of their dreams.

They do not prepare enough for their achievement, so they fall short again and again. Failure becomes the pre-set standard of their self-esteem. Just when they seem to breakthrough or get on top, they blow it.

In truth, the fear of success causes them to procrastinate rather than prepare and take the creative action necessary for success. Rationalization sets in to satisfy the subconscious thought that, *Well you can't expect to get ahead, when you've been through what I have.*

How do we redirect our thinking and help others get through these three fears? One way is through the **development of unshakable self-confidence.** It will open possibilities for you that you can't imagine. You will be able to refigure dreams, set bigger goals, and plunge into life more than ever before.

When your self-confidence becomes unlimited, you will be able to realize more of your potential than you could under any other circumstances. More than 2000 years ago, Aristotle wrote, "*Happiness is a condition.*" It is not something that is achieved by pursuing it directly; rather, it is something that blossoms through our engagement in purposeful activity.

This is a tenet of the **law of indirect effort**. Which claims that almost anything we get in life involving emotional experiences comes to us more indirectly rather than directly. It comes to us as a result of doing something else. If we pursue happiness directly, it eludes us. But if we get busy doing something that is important to us and make progress in the direction of our dreams, we find ourselves feeling very happy.

Self-confidence is also subject to the law of indirect effort. We achieve higher levels by setting and achieving even higher goals and objectives. As we move forward, step by step, once we feel ourselves advancing in life, we feel better and more capable of taking on even more challenges.

We develop a confidence that enables us to tackle larger goals by applying our energies to the accomplishment of smaller goals. We build up our confidence until we get to the point that there is nothing we won't attempt. The habit of setting and achieving larger goals is absolutely indispensable to the development of even higher levels of strength and perseverance.

Successful people believe in their own worth when they have nothing but a dream to hang on to. Why? It is because their *own* self-worth is stronger than the rejection of their ideas by others.

When a person achieves commercial success through the creation of a desired product, he or she is seen as a success. However, it is important to remember that there is just as much value in a person before their product "succeeds" as there is after they made their fortune. Sometimes the fact that he or she has had the courage to move forward against the odds is just as empowering.

Walt Disney was known to ask ten people what they thought of an idea. If they were unanimous in their rejection of it, he would begin to work on it immediately. Of course, he was used to rejection.

Walt dreamed the big dream and for that, children

everywhere will be forever grateful. Was Disney a better man when he was broke and still narrating the original voice of Mickey Mouse? Or was he a better man after he made all those great movies? Or after he built Disneyland? Walt Disney had the self-esteem to keep going when the only reward was his belief in his ideas.

Your job is to take the practical steps to convince yourself objectively that you are absolutely unstoppable and that you can achieve anything. As you systematically and deliberately change your thinking about yourself, your outer reality changes to conform to it. Your thoughts create your life, including—and especially—your thoughts in regard to your level of self-confidence.

The reason why goals are so important is because of several concepts that I refer to as **mental laws**. You are happy and successful to the degree that you align your thoughts with these laws and live in accordance with them.

The first law we already discussed is the law of cause and effect. It is so powerful that you need to keep it in mind at all times. "Whatsoever a man soweth, that so shall he reap." If you *sow* clear goals and objectives in your mind, you will *reap* clear results and rewards in your outer life.

A subset of the law of cause and effect is the **law of attraction**. This is a powerful law in all human interactions, *like attracts like.* You inevitably attract people, ideas, circumstances, and opportunities that are in harmony with your dominant thoughts. Whatever you are thinking most of the time, you are drawing into your life from all directions.

This is why fuzzy goals bring fuzzy results; whereas, clear objectives bring clear results. Since your level of self-confidence is directly tied to how effective you feel you are in achieving your goals, it is critical that you know exactly what it is you want, and that you think of nothing else.

Another law, again a variation of cause and effect, is the **law of correspondence**. This law says that your outer world tends to be a mirror of your inner world. Your outer world of health, wealth, and relationships will be a mirror of your thinking. Your thinking is your most powerful force in your universe. It is both creative and cognitive. Every minute of every day, it is forming the world around you.

Another principle, mentioned earlier, is the law of concentration. This is an important law when it comes to the development and maintenance of your self-confidence. This law says that whatever you dwell upon continually grows into your reality.

Thinking about a subject and dwelling on it continually is like watering and fertilizing a seed. It causes it to grow faster and stronger. The more you dwell, the more of your mental capacities are dedicated to making that goal or subject a reality. Unwavering dedication to a single purpose goes hand in hand with all great accomplishment.

The ability to concentrate without diversion on a single subject to the exclusion of all others, explains why ordinary people achieve extraordinary things. Because of this mental law, the average person with average capabilities, by bringing all of his or her powers to bear on a single goal, can often do far more than a seemingly fortunate person whose energies are weakened by having several goals at once—or no goals at all.

The **law of substitution** states that your conscious

mind can only hold one thought at a time, positive or negative. Whatever thought is held will eventually be accepted by your subconscious mind, and your subconscious mind, in conjunction with all of these laws, will manufacture that thought into reality.

The **law of emotion** propounds that every decision you make, every thought and every action, is based on an emotion of some kind. Your emotion could be based on fear at one end of the spectrum, or desire at the other end. When you hold a thought in your conscious mind and it is charged with an emotion of any kind, it is rapidly accepted by the subconscious mind.

The subconscious mind then activates all the other mental laws to turn that *inner* thought into an *outer* reality. The more powerful the emotion, the more rapid the change will be in your behavior and your experience.

If the emotion is strong enough, the change can be instantaneous. For example, I had a friend, Mike, who smoked for thirty years. Mike claimed he couldn't quit because it was a deep habit from early adulthood. One day he had some chest pains and went to the doctor to have a series of tests done. When the results came in, his doctor told Mike he had a heart problem, and that if he didn't quit smoking, he would die within six months.

Well, the idea of dying was so emotionally charged in my friend, that he took out his cigarettes, threw them in the wastebasket and never touched one again. In a positive vein, if you were absolutely convinced that you were meant to be a great success in life, and there was nothing in the world that could stop you from achieving things, as long as you persisted and threw yourself into every activity whole heartedly, you would become an irresistible force of nature. You can develop this kind of belief, this inner confidence, by developing what is called the **Four C's:**

1) **Clarity** - Knowing exactly what it is that you want and exactly the type of person you wish to become.
2) **Conviction** - Absolutely believing you have the ability to do anything you put your mind to.
3) **Commitment** - The strength to make whatever efforts are necessary.
4) **Consistency** - The depth of character to say and do certain things in a certain manner, until you achieve the goals you set for yourself.

With clarity, conviction, commitment, and consistency, you are on your way to developing the kind of confidence that will make everything possible.

Several years ago, there was a survey done of self-made millionaires. The millionaires varied in age from eighteen to seventy. Their educational backgrounds varied from simple high school diplomas to having as many as two or three PhD's.

The survey revealed a number of characteristics of the self-made millionaires, but all of them had one thing in common: they were able to find the good in life. They had the capacity to look at a person and a situation, regardless of how bad that individual or situation might appear, and find something good. Their focus was on the positive, not the negative.

This emphasizes that a good, healthy mindset forms the foundation for a great attitude. The better your attitude, the healthier your self-esteem. If you really want to find some good in a person or situation, all you have to do is actually *look* for that good.

It is important to keep in mind that your perception of others can greatly impact how you interact with them. There are a few things you should ask yourself:

What kind of kids do you have? What kind of customers, neighbors, and friends surround you? How about your spouse? How do you *see* them and how does this affect how you interact with them? How is the way you treat them affecting their lives, and how does it affect your life?

The effects can be either positive, mediocre, or devastating. No one wants to be mediocre. But even more so, if it's devastating to those around you, it will eventually be even more devastating to you and your life. Our daily lives mold us from the time we are born, so it is imperative that we spend more conscious time reflecting on the effects of what we put in our minds and our bodies, and the effects of what we say and do that our children see and hear.

I read about a study done on a number of school children. The organizers of the study spoke with the teachers who had agreed to participate in the study. They told one teacher that *they were in luck.* They had genius kids who were so smart they were going to know the answers before the teachers even asked the questions. The organizers told them that the students were very bright and were going to excel in everything they did. They then went to another teacher and told that teacher that *they had average kids*. Their students were not hopeless, but they were just average, so they should expect only average results.

By the end of the school year, the "genius" kids were testing at one full grade-level above the students that were labeled as "average." The truth of course was that there were no "genius" kids. They were all average students. The difference in their performance was a direct result of the treatment they received from the teachers, whose preconceptions of the children were formed by what the organizers of the study said.

They continued the study with a new premise. The organizers went to another school and told a teacher that there were six geniuses in his class. They gave him a list with the names of three girls and three boys whom they said were "geniuses." The organizers had actually chosen six students at random who were, in reality, average students.

By the end of the school year, these six "genius" students were excelling in everything they did. Every time one of the "genius" kids asked a question, the teacher would always say things like, "Oh, for someone like you that is no problem." Or, "For someone as smart as you, that will be very easy." The teacher always communicated this way with the six students, reinforcing them that they were intelligent; thus, the students excelled. So, as you can see from this study, we treat people exactly the way we perceive them.

Often when we talk to our children, our spouse, and others that we work with, we criticize them for something they've done. They take it so personally that it goes straight to their heart, and it devastates them. We need to learn to criticize the *performance* and say, "You can do better," instead of criticizing the *performer*. Look at the performer and say, "You can do better than that." Look at the performance and say, "This is not up to your standards." There is an important distinction between those two statements. As I mentioned before, my mother always said, "Never let anyone bring you down to his or her level. Set your own standards. Then live up to those standards."

These stories are an example of how we see the youth of today. We think things like, *They just don't understand. They just don't act the way I hoped they would.* Or, *They are just not taking responsibility for their life and are not going in the direction that I think they should.* But what we really need to be thinking is that most of our children don't control the television programming that comes in over the cable, and they don't own the motion picture companies that release the movies. Nor do they own the other businesses that foster less than ideal habit patterns.

It is the adults that control—or should be controlling—what we put into our children's heads. If we don't take responsibility for molding and nurturing our children, we will never get the ball rolling down the path to a healthy self-image for them. Instead, we will perpetuate the unhealthy life and mindset.

I saw Les Brown speak at a WorldCom sales meeting that I attended in Nashville one year. He said that early on in life he was labeled "uneducably retarded" and was told that he would never learn much in life other than the basics. People were told to not bother teaching him, as it would be a waste of time.

Les said that he was promoted from one grade to the next, just to get him out of each teacher's hair. He said he graduated high school with very little education and was sent out in life to do and be *whatever*.

I have since been to several events where Les was a guest speaker, and I have bought many of his audio and video tapes, and I can tell you that Les has become a very educated man. In fact, Les Brown is one of the most eloquent speakers I have ever heard.

It makes you wonder. How many people have been mislabeled early in life as uneducable and were then treated as such? If you have not already done so, I would encourage you to visit Les Brown's website and buy his audio and video programs. You will see what a great person he has become, because he took control of his own life and took the time to educate himself. The information he presents is fantastic, and his inspirational speaking will give you goose-bumps.

Beliefs are the foundation for creating changes in behavior. In his wonderful book, *Anatomy of an Illness*, Norman Cousins tells an enlightening story about Pablo Casals, one of the greatest musicians of the 20th century.

> *Cousins said that it was almost painful as he watched the old man begin his day. His frailty and arthritis were so debilitating that he needed help with dressing. His emphysema was evident in his labored breathing. He walked with a shuffle, stooped over, hands swollen, and fingers clinched. He looked like a very old, tired man.*
>
> *Even before eating, he made his way to the piano. The piano was one of several instruments on which Casals had become proficient. With great difficulty, he arranged himself on the piano bench. It seemed a terrible*

effort for him to bring his swollen, clenched fingers to the keyboard. But then, something quite miraculous happened. Casals suddenly transformed himself before Cousins' eyes. He went into a ***resourceful state****.*
As he began to play, Casals' physiology changed to such a degree that he began to move and sway and produce, both in his body and on the piano, results that should have been possible for only a healthy, strong, flexible pianist. Cousins remarked that Casals' fingers slowly unlocked the keys like the buds of a plant toward the sunlight. His back straightened and he seemed to breathe more freely.

The very thought of playing the piano changed his whole state and thus the effectiveness of his body. Casals began playing some of Bach's work with great sensitivity and control. He then launched into Brahms' Concerto, and his fingers began to race above the keyboard.

Cousins wrote that Casals' entire body seemed infused with the music. It was no longer stiff and shrunken, but supple and graceful and seemingly free from arthritis. By the time he walked away from the piano, he seemed an entirely different person from the one who sat down to play.

Casals stood straighter and taller, and he walked without the trace of a shuffle. He walked right over to breakfast, ate heartily, and went out for a stroll along the beach.

In the most basic sense, a belief is any guiding faith, or passion that can find great meaning in life. Beliefs are the pre-arranged, organized filters for our perceptions of the world. When we believe something is true, it is like delivering a command to our brain for how to represent what is occurring. Casals believed in music and art. That is what had given beauty and order to his life. That is what still provided daily miracles for him. Because he believed in the transcendent power of his art, he was empowered in a way that almost defied understanding. His beliefs transformed him daily from a tired, old man to a vital genius. In the most profound sense, his belief in his art kept him alive.

John Stuart Mill, the English philosopher, wrote, "One person with a belief is a social power equal to ninety-nine who have only interests." That is precisely why beliefs open the door to excellence.

Beliefs deliver a direct command to your nervous system. Handled effectively, beliefs can be the most powerful forces for creating good in our lives. On the other hand, beliefs that limit your actions and thoughts can be as devastating as resourceful beliefs can be empowering.

Beliefs help us to tap into the richest of resources within us. Beliefs create and direct these resources in support of our desires. In fact, there is no more powerful directing force in human behavior than belief.

Human history is the history of human belief. The people who changed history—Abraham Lincoln, Gandhi, Martin Luther King, Jr.—have all been people who changed our beliefs. To change our behaviors, we have to start changing our beliefs. If we want to model excellence, we need to model beliefs of those who have achieved excellence.

The more we study and learn about human behavior, the more we learn about the extraordinary power that beliefs have over our lives. In many ways, that power defies the logical models most of us have.

A remarkable study was done on schizophrenia. One case involved a woman with a split personality. Typically, her blood sugar levels were completely normal, but when she *believed* she was a diabetic, her whole physiology changed to that of a diabetic. Her belief had become her reality.

There have been numerous studies in which a person in a hypnotic trance is touched by a piece of ice and told that it is a piece of hot metal. Invariably, a blister will develop on contact. What counted was not reality, but belief, or the direct unquestioned communication to the nervous system.

Most of us are aware of the placebo effect. People who are told that a drug will have a certain effect will often experience that effect even when a placebo is given. Norman Cousins, who learned first-hand the power of belief in limiting his own illness, concluded, "Drugs are not always necessary. Belief in recovery always is."

One remarkable placebo study concerned a group of patients with bleeding ulcers. They were divided into two groups. People in the first group were told they were being given a new drug that would absolutely produce relief. Those in the second group were told they were being given an experimental drug, but that very little was known about its effectiveness.

Seventy percent of those in the first group experienced significant relief from their ulcers. Only twenty-five percent of the second group had a similar result. In both cases, patients received a placebo. The only difference was the belief system that they adopted. There are studies of people who have been given drugs with harmful effects, yet they experienced no ill effects when they were told that they would experience a positive outcome.

Studies conducted by Dr. Andrew Weil, a best-selling author and noted physician, have shown that the experiences of drug users correspond almost exactly to their expectations. He found that he could lead a person who had been given amphetamines to feel sedated, or a person given a barbiturate to feel stimulated. The magic of drugs resides in the mind of the user, not in the drug, he concluded. In all these instances, the one constant that powerfully affected the results was belief.

For all its power, there is no abstruse magic involved in the process. Belief is nothing but a state of mind, an internal representation that governs behavior. It is a feeling of certainty about something. If you believe in success, you will be empowered to achieve it. If you believe in failure, those messages will tend to lead you to experience that state as well.

Remember, whether you say you can or can't do something, you are right. Both kinds of beliefs have great power. The question is, *What kinds of beliefs are best to have, and how do we develop them?* I believe the birth of excellence really begins with our awareness that **beliefs are a choice**. We usually don't think of them as a choice, but in fact, we can change our beliefs.

Where do we get our beliefs? Well, there are basically five sources:

1) **The environment we grow up in.** Our environment gives us models of successes and failures, what is right and wrong, and what is possible and impossible. One of the most difficult things for children who grow up in the "projects" is that they see very few positive role models. Without positive role models, it is difficult for them to achieve better results with their life. We see the same challenge in families on the welfare system. In fact, there are often scenarios where there are three or more generations of a family on welfare—all at the same time. As these children grow up, they have few family members who are successful role models. This leads to a lack of belief that there are other choices they can make for their life.
2) **The impact of our life experiences.** Various experiences we have cause us to believe in certain things. When I was growing up, I was fortunate to have my older brothers encourage me to go out and try different things. These new experiences helped me discover things that I had talent for. The successes I had encouraged me to try even more new experiences without fear, and led me to believe that being an accomplished individual was an attainable goal for me.
3) **Knowledge.** What you know and what you don't know both affect your beliefs. If you believe the world is flat, you are going to behave differently than if you know the world is round. Knowledge makes a big difference, so we want to continually educate ourselves with the kind of beliefs that empower us versus those which limit us.

4) **Results we achieved in our past.** If you have attempted to do something in the past and you have succeeded, that nurtures your confidence. On the other hand, if you have attempted something many times without success, you may find it difficult to believe that you can succeed now.
5) **Creating results as we go**. When we set clear goals and begin to experience them as true, we also begin to develop a new set of beliefs that are possible in our lives. Those beliefs can begin to drive us forward.

In my observance of people who have succeeded and achieved excellence, I have found a common belief system. Following is a list of the some of the components of this belief system:

1) They believe that there is no such thing as failure, just results.

Most people have been programmed to fear failure, yet all of us can think of times when we wanted one thing but got another. We have all flunked a test, suffered through bad romances, or put together a business plan, only to see it crumble.

Successful people don't see failure. They don't even believe in failure. In their minds, they always succeed in getting *some* result. When super successful attempt something and do not achieve desired results,they try something else until they obtain their goal.

Successful people move forward, using what they have

learned to take new and different action in order to get new results. Think about it. What is the one asset you have over yesterday? Experience. I feel that I have earned several PhD's in "Life Experience."

For super achievers, there are only results. They are people who take action. Taking action is what sets them apart from mediocrity. The reason they take action is because they don't believe in failure. No matter what happens, they look at an outcome as a result.

If it wasn't the result they intended, they simply learn from the outcome, alter their methods, and take more action. If that doesn't work, they change it again. The trap that most of us fall into is wanting a certain type of result to occur, and feeling like a failure if we don't get that result the first time.

The reality is that there are no failures, because we always succeed in producing *some* result. The outcome just may be different than we planned. As long as you consider a certain outcome to be a failure, you won't be able to tap into your peak level of performance. Whether you are a father, mother, teacher, student, or businessman, peak performance is what we all are striving for. That is where the joy is. Remember, there are no failures, only outcomes.

Belief in failure is poison to the mind. When we store negative emotions and feel like a failure, we affect our physiology and our state of mind. This fear of failure is one of our greatest limitations.

2) Take responsibility.

Responsibility is another attribute that great achievers have in common. No matter what their background or life history, true leaders seem to share the belief that they are the source—the creator. On some level, they generated the outcome, if not by their physical actions, then by their mental actions. They believe that they create whatever happens in their life. If someone cut them off on the road, they contributed to that outcome in some way. Maybe they were driving in the other car's blind spot, or they weren't paying close enough attention, or they didn't anticipate the lane change of a car. That is how leaders are—they take full responsibility.

This is not how most people respond in our culture. Most people believe that they are the victims. They believe that most events are often beyond their control. These are the same people who see themselves as failing on a consistent basis. I would rather believe that I can affect the outcome, because when I feel that I am in control, then I will take the action to make a difference.

I want to challenge you to adopt this belief for your life. No matter what happens, you create it. The truth is that leaders operate from this mindset. The key point to remember is that we are in charge. Although some things may seem like they are happening *to* us, if we adopt the belief that we are in control, then we can change the results. If we can change the results, then we can create the life of our dreams.

3) People are your greatest resource.

Individuals of excellence, universally have a great sense of respect and appreciation for others. They have a sense of team and unity. They realize that there is no long lasting success unless we have significant communication with others. The way to succeed is to form a successful team that is working together.

In Japanese factories, workers and management often eat in the same cafeteria. Both groups have input in evaluating their team performance. Their success reflects the wonders that can be achieved when we respect people, rather than try to manipulate them. Unlike many of the beliefs we've discussed, this one is easier to *talk about*, than to actually adopt. It is easy to pay lip service to the idea of treating people with the kind of respect that they deserve. It isn't always easy to do it.

As you move through your life, keep in mind the constant desire to treat people with love, respect, and appreciation. Do people feel respected by me? If they don't, change your behaviors until they do.

4) Work is play.

Do you know any person who has achieved massive success by doing something that they hate? I don't. One of the keys to success is making a successful marriage between what you do and what you love to do. Maybe we can't paint as well as Michelangelo, but what we *can* do is try our best to find work that invigorates and excites us.

We can bring many aspects of what we do at *play* to

what we do at *work*. Researchers are discovering surprising things about workaholics. They seem manically focused on work because they love it. Work challenges them and makes their life richer.

These people tend to look at work the way most of us look at play. They see it as a way to personally stretch and learn new things. By adopting this kind of attitude, you will change the quality of your life. You must enrich your world and your work with the same vitality and curiosity that you bring to your play.

5) Enduring success cannot exist without commitment.

Individuals who succeed have a belief and power in commitment. They believe that there is no great success without commitment.

If you *know* your outcome, then in order to achieve it, model what works, take action, sharpen your sensory acuity, and continue refining your direction to ensure you stay on the right path. Remember, success leaves clues. Study those who succeed.

I love the mindset of happiness, and I believe it is a choice. Zig Ziglar says that *we must feed our mind every day, just as we feed our bodies*. We would never go a day without eating, at least not if we can help it. If we do, we are hungry and ornery. In that same vein, if we don't *feed* our minds every day, our mind becomes hungry. Just as we get ornery when we don't eat, we get irritable when we don't feed our minds with healthy, positive input.

Mastering a healthy self-image is the cornerstone for

true happiness and contentment, as well as the foundation for empowerment and success. Zig Ziglar has said that *regardless of where you have come from, you can and do grow each day*. Tony Robbins adds: "The past does not equal the future." We all must set out on a journey to master a healthy self-image so that we can have the happiness that will help empower us for greatness. Not just for ourselves, but also for the betterment of everyone we touch each day.

Life can be a vicious circle of negativity and unhappiness; or, with the proper training, it can be an exciting upward spiral of joyous fulfillment. But we must consciously make that choice. I realize that there is no overnight success; there is no way to make any journey without some roadblocks and detours.

It is important that we start building a map for your journey. We are going to layout the map with the proper road signs to reach the goal of mastering your healthy self-image.

The number one step in building a healthy self-image is to **learn to smile**. This may sound simplistic, but we must learn to smile from the inside out. Your smile must not only radiate from your mouth, but also from your eyes, and even more so, from your heart.

The more you smile, the more it will become a habit. Of course, learning to smile takes practice, as does any habit. It will immediately make you feel better, and the more you smile, the deeper your feeling of contentment. In my daily life, I talk about smiling often, because I believe it is a key foundation for happiness and contentment.

Self-Talk and Mastering Your Mind

How many of us talk to ourselves? The answer is *everyone.*

Psychologists estimate that we think around fifty-thousand thoughts a day. Assuming we are sleeping at least seven hours a day, that's roughly three thosand thoughts an hour. Many of these thoughts are about ourselves: *What's wrong with me? I should have said that differently. I don't look good in this dress. I am not smart enough. I will never get the job I want.* And one that a lot of people are thinking right now is, *The economy is a mess.*

We often don't realize it, but negative thoughts and voicing negative comments are damaging our mindset. They create a negativity that echoes in our head. If we think negative thoughts all day long, it affects us adversely.

What we need to be saying to ourselves is: *I like myself. I love the way I care about others. I am awesome at__________* (fill in the blank). I have a small plastic hanger hanging on my bathroom mirror that reads:

I like myself, I love my life, I am excited, I am happy, I am healthy, and I add brightness to the life of everyone I meet.

I give this same hanger out to people so they can have the quote to read to themselves everyday as they look in the mirror.

I would love to hear you say these words to yourself every morning, as you get dressed for your day. This will change your life and set you on a course that will make you unstoppable.

When people ask you how you are doing, start saying, "Awesome! How about you?" I know when I first considered saying this to someone, I felt embarrassed and wasn't sure I could pull it off. But I practiced saying it to myself, which gave me the nerve to voice it and it went okay. Within a few weeks, I was saying it all the time.

Now I never hesitate to answer, "How are you doing?" with, "Awesome! How about you?" Try it, say it over and over again until it feels comfortable. This self-talk will be life-changing, and at the same time, you will be letting the world around you know how different you are becoming. Don't forget to say it with a big smile. This will increase the effect ten-fold.

Two important things we must learn to control are our self-talk and what we visualize, in our minds. I heard Denis Waitley talk about watching the Olympics in Seoul, South Korea. He mentioned Greg Louganis, the American gold medal.

Louganis did a back dive during the competition and hit his head on the diving board. They replayed the incident over and over. The people who filmed it asked Greg if he would like to see the video. He told them there was no way he wanted to allow a negative image like that to get into his mind. He said that he didn't want to give credence to the possibility that he would hit is head on the diving board. This is the focus of a winner.

You need to be conscious of everything that you see and hear. If you watch TV all the time, and wallow in all the negativity in the dramas and reality shows (whose producers feel they need the negativity to keep your attention), you will invariably pump more and more negativity into your mind . Even the comedy shows use negativity in many of the jokes they make about how "stupid" something—or someone—is.

If you are going to build your self-esteem, all this negative media is not what you need to put into your mind. If you watch informational and educational TV, or watch videos with a healthy and educational format, such as those by Zig Ziglar, Tony Robbins, Les Brown, Brian Tracy, Earl Nightingale, Denis Waitley, among others, then you will be on the fast-track to a healthy self-esteem.

According to the UCLA Brain Research Institute, the potential of the human brain to create, store, and learn may be virtually unlimited. We could, without any difficulty, learn forty languages, memorize a set of encyclopedias from A to Z, and complete the required courses of dozens of colleges. If this is true—and I think it is—why don't more people learn and accomplish more in their lives?

One obvious, but painful reason is that they don't

believe they are worth that much time and effort. Their self-esteem is so low, they don't see that they deserve the benefits that come from the learning and accomplishment, and so they quit before they ever get started.

They have been told many times that they are lazy, which also keeps them from making the effort. People condition themselves to doing only what is absolutely necessary to get by. The only way we can gain knowledge is by studying. Unfortunately, for most people, studying is like paying taxes or going to the dentist, so they avoid it.

Most people believe that graduation day is the end of their need to study. Today, more than ever, the world is full of the most abundant supply of free educational materials. Our libraries and universities, and of course the Internet, are all filled with enough data on every subject to make anyone who is willing to spend one hour per night both intelligent and successful.

Peter Drucker, the famed management expert, advises us that today, more than ever, **knowledge is power**. It controls access to unlimited opportunity and advancement. Scientists, scholars, and computer geeks are no longer on the lower pay scale they were at one time. They are largely in charge of the information, and not only have they changed the world as we knew it, but they are also on the verge of providing us with ongoing dramatic changes. Just as the industrial revolution catered to line managers with manufacturing and materials experience, so the information revolution calls for intellectual entrepreneurs with strong technical and financial educations.

One of the best kept secrets to success is that of possessing a large vocabulary. This type of proficiency implies broad, general knowledge and suggests a more successful person, regardless of their occupation.

Knowledge is the frontier of tomorrow. Our struggle for physical control may not be as crucial right now, and even in the future, as our ability to survive and co-exist intellectually amid all of the fallout of the technological progress.

One of the major issues we have in trying to work with each other toward mutually beneficial solutions, lies in our ability to express our thoughts in words. Frustrations with this inability often result in physical violence. While violence has been increasing each year, the nation's vocabulary level has been decreasing approximately one percentage point each year. Regardless of education, people use only about four hundred words in more than eighty percent their every day conversation. There are over 450,000 words in an unabridged dictionary, yet we use the same words over and over again. If we were only to learn ten new words each day for one year, we would become some of the most learned and well-spoken individuals in the world.

Reading and listening are the best ways to gain greater knowledge in vocabulary. As you continue to learn, you will become more aware of your natural talents and skills. You can then develop those talents and skills as you read and listen, so that you will be able to express your ideas more clearly. The more education you receive, the happier you will become.
Never stop reaching.

Here are ten action steps towards knowledge:

1) Continue educating yourself regardless of your age.

Studies indicate that older adults do better in classes than the younger students.

2) When you read, always keep a dictionary next to you. If you look up the meaning on the spot, it becomes easier to remember.

3) Establish a good vocabulary primer. Approximately 3500 words separate the average person from those with the best vocabularies. Read to your children from a young age, even before their first birthdays. They will assimilate more than you can imagine. Encourage your children to read more than they watch TV or play video games.

4) Consider taking a reputable aptitude test. Check with the school or your local library.

5) Before you make a decision, ask yourself, *Is this the honest thing to do? How will this affect others?*

6) Check the aptitudes of your children by their sophomore year in high school. By the 11th grade, they should be deciding which college they would like to attend, or the first job they are going to have. By helping them discover their natural gifts, you are giving them a fishing pole they can use to fish with for the rest of their lives. Don't press your children to choose the same career you did, unless *they* have determined they want to enter your chosen field.

7) Think, say, and do what you believe is true—consistently.

8) Make sure you have high-speed Internet access, if it is available in your area.

9) Don't overlook correspondence courses, seminars, and night or weekend classes. There are also audio and video home study courses that are outstanding.

10) Model yourself after people you most admire and respect, and above all, set a model of integrity and sincerity for your children and others who look up to you.

So what causes some men and women to succeed while others of similar intelligence don't? What are the necessary ingredients that set the super successful apart from the rest of society? Tony Robbins calls it "personal power." I call it **desire**.

Desire is absolutely imperative for any kind of success, and the more desire you have, the more success you will garner. Desire creates the personal power and gives you the ability to take action. This is what separates the winners from those who only wish for success.

Those who have the ability to take action "in spite of it all" are those who make their dreams a day-to-day reality. No matter how aligned we think we are, we all still have challenges and difficulties. The winner is the one who can anticipate the challenges and figure out how to use them to their advantage.

Success leaves clues. People who succeed do certain things over and over again. If you are wise and pay attention to what they do consistently, and you do likewise, you will produce similar results.

Success is not an accident. The difference between the people who produce positive results and those who don't is that successful people follow consistent, logical patterns that are specific pathways to excellence. We all can learn to follow those logical patterns and unleash the magic within us.

I have always been fascinated by why some people, in spite of all the advantages in life, barely get by; yet others who have faced great odds, turn those obstacles into tremendous opportunities and transform their lives. You are going to be able to change any emotion within you, you are going to learn to take your fears of rejection, failure, and success, and the unknown, and turn them into positive anticipation. Not just through positive thinking alone, but by adding positive programming as well.

You are going to learn to create instant rapport with anyone you meet. I am sure you have met someone and instantly felt connected to him or her, as if you already knew them. I will show you how you can create that feeling consistently.

As I reflected on my life, I realized that personal power and the ability to take action consistently toward my goals were significant reasons that I was succeeding while others were not. I began to study successful people to see if they had a common formula for success, and I discovered that they do.

They all seem to **know their outcome**. They have a reason, almost an obsession, for making their goals happen. **If you don't know what you want, how will you ever get it?** We all have this incredible "computer"(our brain) yet we rarely make good use of it. We don't do a good job of "programming" the computer, so we don't get the desired results.

Another trait successful people share is their **ability to take action**. If you know what you want and don't do anything about it, then it is just a dream. It will never be a reality. Action is the only thing that translates dreams into reality. Those who consistently take action will always gravitate towards success.

If you look around and see people who are succeeding, you may do what I have done. I used to look at super successful people and think, *Yeah, well they are just lucky, or have a certain amount of talent*. But, in reality, when you look closer, you discover that it wasn't that they had it so easy, or that they were gifted; rather, it was that they knew what they wanted, and they took action—and kept going until they discovered what it took to succeed.

A great example is the story of Colonel Sanders and his restaurant, Kentucky Fried Chicken. The Colonel overcame some tremendous obstacles. He didn't have much of an education, certainly not one that would have taught him how to grow a large franchise. He didn't have any real marketing experience. And he certainly didn't start with a huge bank account.

He made the whole thing happen starting with one resource: desire. He knew what he wanted and got himself to take action. At the age of sixty-five, he received his first Social Security check for $105. He looked at the check and told himself that he was not going to live like this—so he took action.

The Colonel asked himself, "What resources do I have?" He knew he had a chicken recipe that a lot of people liked, and he came up with an idea. He would share his chicken recipe with restaurant owners. He believed his chicken was so good that it was sure to help the restaurants increase their sales. All he would ask from them was a percentage of the profits that they earned from his recipe. With this in mind, he went out and took his idea to the streets—unlike many people who don't follow through.

Have you ever had an idea for something? Something that you thought everyone in the world would clamor for until they possessed it. Have you ever walked into a store six months after you thought of that idea, only to find your idea on the shelf because someone "stole" it? What was the difference between them and you? Was it intelligence? No. The difference was, they action. That is what Colonel Sanders did. He went out and knocked on his first restaurant door and gave his pitch. He told them he had the best recipe in the world and wanted to give it to them, and they didn't have to pay for the recipe—just give him a percentage of their increased profits on all the chicken they sold.

As you can imagine, there wasn't a whole lot of enthusiasm on the other side of the counter. The restaurant owner basically said, "No thanks. I already have a chicken recipe."

The impressive thing about Colonel Sanders—or anyone who succeeds—is that he knew his outcome. He knocked on another door, and another, and was rejected time after time. But each time he was rejected, he took into account another key to success: **sensory acuity**. Not only did the Colonel know his outcome, not only did he take action, but he also had sensory acuity.

He understood and paid attention to the effect of his present actions to see whether they were moving him closer to or further away from his goals. Every time he got a result, even if it wasn't the one he wanted, he tried to learn from that result, make an adjustment, and use the final piece of the success formula: **change your approach**.

He learned from what happened and changed his approach; always remembering what he wanted, taking action, learning from what he got, and changing his approach when the situation called for it. Over and over again.

Do you know how many "no's" he got before he got his first "yes"? He got 1009 "no's" before he got his first "yes." How many of you, after just a few "no's" would give up? How many of you can honestly say that after even a hundred "No thanks", would you have continued knocking on those doors?

The point is this: this man had the ability to get himself to do whatever it took. He had command of his own emotions, his own behaviors, and most importantly, his own mind. He spent two years traveling, being rejected time after time. He learned from each situation, made adjustments, and continued to work toward his goal.

This method of learning is much like the way a pilot operates when flying from Los Angeles to Hawaii. Getting there requires sensory acuity. Did you know that an airplane on its flight to Hawaii is off course approximately ninety percent of the time? The plane takes off in the direction of Hawaii, but it often hits an air pocket or wind, blowing it off course. The plane must make an adjustment to get it back on track.

Fortunately, the pilot has a computer on board that puts the plane back on track. Success in human terms is very similar. We don't just go straight to our goal. That isn't how life works. We have an outcome in mind, and we get ourselves to take action until the mission is accomplished.

A primary component of power in our society is **communication**. At the dawn of civilization, power was measured in physiological terms. He who was the strongest had *power* and was in control of life and the community. As man progressed, power became based on hierarchies, on Kings and Queens, for example. Those who wanted power in their lives would try to develop some of that power through their association with royalty. When the industrial age came, capital was power. It was capital that allowed people to build and change.

But today, we are in a communication age. We are in an era when information is coming to us at an incredible pace and those who can master human communication, both the communication they have with themselves and with others, are in the true position of power.

The quality of our life is defined by the quality of our communication. It is a simple statement, yet profoundly true. The way you communicate with yourself, your "self-talk", determines the way you experience life. Who must you first master the art of communication with, if you really want to be happy and joyous in life? Yourself.

For most people, when things happen in their lives, they tend to believe that "everything happens for a reason," and they see it as a "sign" that is leading them somewhere. But I don't believe this is true. For everything that happens in life, the meaning of it is however we interpret it.

How many times have you heard these statements? *Well, I guess it was meant to be*. Or, *Things happen for a reason, so I just have to accept the outcome as it is*. Oftentimes we get caught up in what the environment teaches us or what our friends tell us, but ultimately we decide the meaning of an experience. Too often we operate on "automatic pilot," but we must take ownership of it.

For example, let's say you are in a relationship, and

your partner leaves you. There are two ways of handling this experience, and which way you choose to handle the experience is determined by how you communicate with yourself.

You can say, "Oh gosh, they left me because I'm worthless." Or you can say, "Hallelujah! I am free of that miserable situation." How you communicate with yourself will ultimately determine the life you experience. One person feels sad and doesn't know which way to turn, while the other person feels fantastic and says, "What's next? Let's get on with it!"

The key is learning to communicate well with ourselves. The funny thing is that we all have this strange illusion that when people really succeed on a massive scale, especially economically, that they are happy, and everything is great in their life. The reality, however, is often far from that. Some of the most powerful, successful people in the world today have major personal problems, because they haven't mastered the skill of communicating with themselves. Many people have achieved success in the outside world by communicating with others in a way that causes the other person to respond. Unfortunately, even though they have mastered communicating with the *outside* world, they haven't mastered communicating with their *inside* world. This is why "externally" successful people like Janis Joplin and Jimi Hendrix end up destroying their lives. They haven't mastered internal communication. You have to master them both, so that no matter what experiences you have, you are in charge, and you are happy.

Zig Ziglar says, "You can get everything in life you want if you will just help enough other people get what they want." The only way that is going to happen is if you learn to communicate effectively. Communication is the ultimate power. The quality of our lives is the manner of our communication with ourselves and with others.

How do you direct your emotions and behaviors so that no matter what happens in life, you are in charge? We'll start with, *How did I change my life*? Well, I started with changing how I communicated with myself. When I was younger, I communicated with myself in a negative way, putting myself down, and telling myself I was not capable of much of anything. I was not using my body or my facial expressions in a manner that showed I was in control of my life. I was moving in a very limp, lazy, despondent way. As a result, that was how I felt in my body. Those were the kinds of results I was producing.

What emotions and behaviors do people need to be in control of their lives?

1) **Passion.** All successful people have discovered a reason, a consuming, energizing, almost obsessive purpose that drives them to do and to grow. It gives them the fuel that powers their "success train" and causes them to tap their true potential. It is passion that causes people to stay up late and get up early. Passion gives life power, excitement, and meaning. There is no greatness without a passion to *be* great. It doesn't matter who we are, we all come to realize that the key to our success is finding something that mobilizes us, something that gives us an obsessive desire to create our lives exactly how we see them.
2) **Belief.** People who succeed on a major scale differ greatly in their beliefs from those who just exist. Our beliefs about

who we *are* and what we *can* be determine what we *will* be. If we believe in magic, we will live a magical life. If we believe our life is defined by narrow limits, then we will inevitably make those limits real. Many people are passionate, but because of their limiting beliefs about who they are and what they can do, they never take the actions that can turn their dreams into reality.

Now, passion and belief provide the fuel that pushes us toward excellence, but that is not enough. If it were, it would be enough to fuel a rocket and send it flying blindly toward space. In addition to "fuel," we need a destination. We need an intelligent sense of logical progression to succeed in reaching a target. We also need a strategy.

3) **Strategy**. Strategy is a way of organizing our resources. When Steven Spielberg decided to be a filmmaker, he mapped out a course that would lead to the world he wanted to conquer. He figured out what he wanted to learn, whom he needed to know, and what he needed to do. Spielberg had a passion and a belief, but he also had a strategy that would make those qualities work to his greatest potential. Every great entertainer, politician, parent, or employer knows that it is not enough just to have the resources to succeed. One must also use those resources in the most effective way. A strategy is the recognition that the best talents and ambitions need to find the right avenue. **You can open a door by breaking it down, or you can find the key that opens it.**

4) **Clarity of Values.** What makes America great? Patriotism, pride, a sense of tolerance, and a love of freedom. These things are values—the fundamental, ethical, moral judgments about what is most important in our lives. They are specific belief systems that we have about what is right and wrong for our lives. Many people don't have a clear idea about what is most important to them. Many times, people do things that they regret afterward. In contrast, people who are great successes are people with a clear, fundamental sense about what is right and what really matters. They all have different visions, but what they have in common is a fundamental, moral grounding—a sense of who they are and why they do what they do.

Passion is affected by our beliefs. The more we believe we can accomplish something, the more we are willing to invest in its achievement. Yet belief by itself is not enough to achieve excellence. It's a good start, but if you believe you are going to see the sun rise, and your strategy is to look to the west, you will be disappointed. If your strategy for success causes you to do things that don't fit your belief system then even the best strategy won't work. This is often seen in individuals who begin to succeed only to end up sabotaging their own success. Their problem is they have an internal conflict between what they value internally and what their strategy is for achieving external success.

5) **Bonding Power**. All four of the above specifics are inseparable from this trait. Successful people have an extraordinary ability to bond with others. They have the

ability to connect with and develop rapport with people from a variety of backgrounds and beliefs. Sure, there is the occasional mad genius that comes up with something that changes the world, but the genius spends a good deal of their time alone; they see success on one level, but not on many others. The great successes of our culture and our world all have the ability to form bonds that unite them with millions of others.

The greatest success is not on the stage of the world. It is in the deepest recesses of your own heart. Everyone needs to form a lasting, loving bond with others. Without that, any success is hollow. We want to *feel* the success that comes from connecting with people we meet. Bonding power comes from caring deeply for others and is a skill that anyone can develop. It is a skill that will allow you to tap into higher levels of success than you ever imagined before.

6) **Mastery of Communication**. This is the essence of everything that we have talked about so far, and everything that we will talk about in the future. The way we communicate with others and the way we communicate with ourselves ultimately determines the quality of our lives. People who succeed in life are those who have learned to take any challenge and process that experience in a way that enables them to successfully change. People who fail accept adversities in life as limitations. People who shape our lives and our cultures are also masters of communication with others. What they have in common is

the ability to communicate a quest, a joy, and a vision to others. Mastery of communication is what makes a great parent, a great teacher, or a great businessperson.

Being mentally "fit" requires the use of some techniques. The first mental fitness technique is that of **positive self-talk**. The way you talk to yourself has a huge impact on your thinking and feeling. Many researchers have discovered that high performing men and women talk to themselves differently than low performing men and women. Your inner dialogue sets the tone of your emotional life. You are happy or sad, positive or negative, depending on how you talk to yourself and how you interpret events in your life. For example, if you are cut off in traffic and immediately become angry, thinking how stupid and irresponsible the other driver is, you will have a very different reaction than if you empathize with the other person, thinking that he or she must be late or distracted, or must not have seen you. The *external* event is the same, but your interior conversation will determine whether or the experience is positive or negative.

The starting point of using positive self-talk is to interpret everything that happens to you in a favorable way. Become what W. Clement Stone called an "inverse paranoid." Imagine that the whole world is in a giant conspiracy to help you become successful and happy. Just as a paranoid is convinced that there is a conspiracy *against* him or her, an inverse paranoid is convinced that there is a conspiracy *for* him or her.

In his book, *Think and Grow Rich*, Napoleon Hill says that a prime characteristic of the most successful people is that they always look for the benefit within every setback or obstacle. The **law of substitution** states that if you are looking into every difficult situation for a lesson, or the possibility it might contain, your mind tends to remain positive, and you continue to function at your very best. Whenever you think of a person or event, talk to yourself in a positive language. The most powerful of all affirmations for building self-confidence is for you to repeat over and over, "I can do it."

These simple words are the verbal antidote to the fear of failure, which is the great destroyer of self-confidence, and probably the main reason for most failures in life. You can diminish the fear of failure by repeating, "I can do it." The most powerful affirmation for building self-esteem is, "I like myself." These simple words, repeated with enthusiasm, are eventually accepted by your subconscious. As you accept this message, your self-esteem increases. Accordingly, your ability to perform and your level of effectiveness improve in every aspect of life. If you want to do your work better, just say, "I love my job."

In their book, *Success Through a Positive Attitude*, Napoleon Hill and W. Clement Stone recommend that you repeat several times day, " I feel happy, healthy, and terrific." You will find it hard to worry while repeating this kind of positive message to yourself.

Your potential is unlimited when you draw on affirmations. By repeating affirmations, you can install powerful commands that will eventually determine your automatic response, feelings, and actions.

There are several techniques you can use to drive

affirmations into your subconscious. The first technique is referred to as the **Three P's**: affirmations must be in the **present** tense, they must be **positive**, and they must be **personal**. The affirmations, "I can do it, I like myself, I feel terrific," all said in the present tense, are positive and personal.

The subconscious is very literal and responds best to present tense. You can create affirmations for each of your goals and by repeating these affirmations continually, you will drive them deep into your subconscious. Before long you will find yourself completely motivated and determined to achieve them.

The second technique is to **write out your goals in the form of affirmations**. Write them in large black letters and re-read them, reciting the affirmations several times each day. This strategy, and every other technique you employ to convince yourself that your goals are achievable, will help to increase your self-esteem and self-confidence. This approach will help you to take the specific actions that will make your goals a reality.

The third technique that helps affirmations is **positive visualization**. This is creating clear mental pictures of the person you want to be and the things you want to do. Your subconscious mind cannot tell the difference between a real experience and one you vividly imagine. What determines the impact of visualization is the amount of emotion you mix with the picture when you hold these images in your conscious mind. Positive emotion will create an uplifting response in your subconscious.

The more emotion with which you visualize, the faster the picture will crystallize. This mode of visualization for a peak performance is called **mental rehearsal**. You go through an upcoming event in your mind, seeing it in perfect detail over and over, with you being successful in the end. Prior to any event, you recall and relive a previous experience of excellent performance.

Take a few minutes to replay in your mind a picture of the last time you did this successfully. For example, if you have to make a sales call, take a few moments before your meeting to close your eyes and see yourself in the sales call. Imagine you are relaxed, calm, and in complete control. See the prospect or customer responding positively or signing the contract at the end of your visit. If you have an interview, take a few minutes to rehearse the interview in your mind. Go through every part of it and see yourself performing at your very best. Visualize the other person responding in a positive way.

Flood your mind with pictures and sensations of the reality that you want to experience. If you want to live in a nicer home, then go to Open Houses in the neighborhoods you want to reside. Don't worry about whether buying the house is possible, or how high the price is. Your primary job is to get the picture clearly in your mind. Practice the law of concentration by allowing your mind to dwell on the things you want, and most importantly, feel the feelings you would feel as you have this in your life.

The key to activating your mental powers through affirmation and visualization is for you to imagine how you would feel if you had already achieved your goal. Imagine the feelings of pride, happiness, that you would savor as a result of obtaining your objective. This emotional component is the catalyst that causes the other components to work more rapidly.

One of the best methods I have seen for programming

your mind is the "end of the movie exercise." It is very simple. Imagine you go to a movie, and when you arrive at the theatre, you find out there are ten minutes left in the previous showing of the movie. Instead of waiting in the lobby for your show, you decide to go in and watch the last ten minutes of the previous screening. You see the plot unfold, the drama resolved and the movie end. When the movie starts again, you watch it from the beginning. You *now* know, however, that it has a happy ending. Instead of becoming caught up in the drama, you relax peacefully, knowing the outcome. You can apply this same approach to everything you do. You can manufacture your own level of self-confidence by imagining that no matter what the situation, things turn out perfectly in the end. Prior to a meeting, interview, etc., take a few moments to get that "end of the movie feeling," and then just relax. No matter what happens in the interim, you already know the result.

The fourth technique for solidifying affirmations is to **continually feed your mind with books, magazines, and CDs filled with positive messages**. Just as you become what you eat, you also become what you think. Everything that you allow into your conscious mind is either raising or lowering your self-esteem and confidence.

This brings me to the fifth and final technique for strengthening affirmations: **surround yourself with positive people and avoid negative people**. Discipline yourself to remove the negative people from your life. Because we are so influenced by the people we spend time with, we must do everything possible to ensure that we are surrounded by the kind of people we want to be like. This concept is so crucial that research has shown that habitual association with critical, complaining people can be enough by itself to sabotage all your chances for happiness and success.

You can begin to change your social environment by thinking about the kind of people you admire and want to be like. Read about people who are "going somewhere" with their lives. Identify with winners mentally. When you do, you will notice a subtle change in your mentality and you'll begin to attract winners in *your* life. At the same time, you will activate the **law of repulsion** and negative people will start to drift away from you. Very quickly, your relationships, both personal and professional, will start to change for the better.

If all these ideas seem like a lot of trouble, remember the reality principle that both actions and inactions have consequences. Remember, whatever you sow, or fail to sow, is going to determine what you reap in the end. If you act in a manner consistent with the qualities of high performance and self-confidence, those actions will generate feelings consistent with these qualities.

Every positive action you take in the direction of your dreams and goals will reinforce your belief in yourself and your ability to achieve. Develop a sense of urgency and move quickly when an opportunity presents itself. A fast tempo is essential for success. The faster you move, the better you feel.

The world can be divided into two categories: the **talkers** and the **doers**. The world is full of talkers who are convinced that if they talk about something enough, it is the same as if they actually do it. But *you* know that it is all just hot air. You want to be a doer, a person who will not only dream their goals, but also act on them.

Here are seven action steps to boost your creativity:

1) **Daydream Your Future.** Be optimistic about the future and be open to alternatives. When you daydream, focus on the future, not on the past. Acquire the ability to recognize and break your bad habits. You are an independent thinker and have a constructive discontent with the status quo, so reinforce these feelings about yourself.
2) **Relax.** Learn a relaxation technique that works for you. Your creative imagination can be pre-played and re-played best when you are relaxed. Try my idea of sitting in a dark room for thirty minutes to an hour a few times a week.
3) **Visualize in First Person.** When you visualize yourself as already accomplishing one of your goals, make certain that you visualize the image from the perspective of seeing it out of *your* eyes. Don't visualize the image as though you were a spectator. Using this perspective is very important.
4) **Forgive Yourself.** Don't scold or berate yourself when you make a mistake.
5) **Problems are Opportunities**. Recognize and approach problems creatively. It is best to view problems and situations as opportunities to grow. So change your view toward problems.
6) **Make Educated Decisions.** When making decisions, use the old Ben Franklin method: do your pros and cons list. In the *pros* column, list all the advantages, benefits, and positive results if you went forward with the decision.

In the *cons* column, list all the disadvantages, losses, and negative results if you chose another path. Study the possible impact of each column. If the advantages outweigh the disadvantages, and if you can live with the consequences as well as the positive benefits, then go forward with the decision.

7) **Touch the world.** Take time out to ride your bike or walk in the sand. We need to explore the wonderful, right-brained world of the creative child within. Do it soon!

I've talked about using communication as a means of inspiring yourself to take action. What other methods can we use to spur us into action? What is the element that makes the difference in the *quality* of how you behave and how you feel? The element that makes a difference is your **state of mind**. Your state of mind and emotions will determine how much of your personal power is available to you.

Have you ever watched your beloved team win a game against a noted rival. When your team won, you got excited, but thirty minutes later, you were thinking about something else. A month later, you then watched your team win a conference championship. This time, you were so excited that you decided to go to an After Party that night, and you found yourself still talking about the game a week later.

The basic events—the team winning a game—were the same in many respects. But in one scenario, you were just reasonably happy, while in the other scenario you were so excited, it took a week to get through all the celebration. Why did you exhibit such varied behavior in such similar situations?

Your behavior was the result of the state of mind you were in at that time. That state of mind was the generator, or governor, of your behavior. Your behavior is always a product of the state of mind you find yourself in.

What creates your state of mind? Basically two things. One component is **physiology**, which is how you carry your body. The manner in which you use your body—your posture, your breathing pattern—can determine your biochemical functioning. If you are sitting with a slumped over posture, breathing very shallowly, and speaking softly and meekly, do you really think you are going to be feeling motivated? When you are physically run down, do you not respond differently than you do when you are energized? So physiology tremendously affects our state of mind and our behavior.

The other factor that has a profound impact on your state of mind is the way your mind interprets the outside world. We call this way of thinking our **internal representation**. This visualization "represents" what is going on inside your mind, or what you picture, and how you picture it; what your self-talk is and how you say it; the kind of tone in which you verbalize the interior dialogue.

If you feel physically vibrant; consequently, you see the world differently. If you perceive the world differently, it changes your vibrancy. Surely you have found yourself in a situation where something catches your attention (changes your vibrancy), and suddenly you feel physically strong and energetic.

So these two dynamics work together on what we call a cybernetic loop. If you change one, the other changes automatically. They are linked together. Ideally, you want to change them simultaneously, so that they support one another, and put you in a state of mind that will enable you to produce the kind of behavior you want. If you learn to control the way you represent things mentally, as well as the way in which you use your body, you can direct any aspect of your life.

If you want to change how you feel and behave, then change the way you use your physiology. For example if you are feeling depressed, but you stand up straight, puff your chest out, and put a smile on your face, you won't feel depressed any longer. Scientists have verified this. People have beaten lie detectors by putting themselves in a physiological state, posture, and breathing pattern similar to that of when they are telling the truth. As a result, they *believe* that they are telling the truth and fool the lie detector test. Why not reprogram yourself by changing how you use your body and your thought processes?

I am convinced that if we were to consciously take the time to stand up straight, puff our chest out, and wear a smile on our face throughout the day, we would change our mindset and our lives almost immediately. You have all the resources you need to succeed in your life. The question is, *Can you get yourself to take action on this mindset?*

Don't forget this affirmation: *I like myself, I love my life, I am excited, I am happy, I am healthy, and I add brightness to the life of everyone I meet*. Please repeat often.

Building That Healthy Self Image

Play a game with me. Let's pretend your telephone rings and it's a well-respected friend. You know this person very well and you trust and respect his opinion.

He says, "Hey Pat, I should have told you this years ago, but I'm just calling to let you know that I think you are one of the nicest people that has ever drawn a breath of air. You are an asset to this community and someone that I like to be around. You mentally challenge and stimulate me, and I get excited with ideas every time we're together. If I could just spend a half an hour a day with you, there is no telling what I could accomplish."

If you had gotten a call like this in the morning, what kind of a day would you have had? If you made a sales call that day, would you make a better presentation? If you were a surgeon, would you do a better job of operating? If you were a teacher, would you connect better with your students? Would you be better at whatever you did that day?

Here is the question: How much more would you know about being a sales person, a surgeon, or a teacher? Obviously you would not know any more than you did before you got the call. Yet there is no doubt that you would perform better at everything that day, because your image of yourself would have changed.

Your performance will mirror the image you have of yourself. There will never be another you. You are the rarest thing in existence. And because of your rarity, you are surely valuable.

Want to improve your self-image?

Make a "victory list." Take inventory of your talents and your best qualities. When you are down, or nothing is going your way, take out your victory list to remind yourself: *I have accomplished many things in my life. I am a great person*. As you reflect on these accomplishments, your self-image continues to build.

Want to improve your self-image?

Dress up. Get rid of the stale items in your wardrobe and treat yourself to a new look. Make-up and dress up, if you want to go up.

Want to improve your self-image?

Learn to smile more often each day. One of the most important foundation stones of happiness and self-esteem is a beeming smile. The bigger your smile, the happier you are. The act of smiling establishes a mental attitude of happiness. Not only does it release endorphins, but it is also infectious. This interaction subconsciously enhances your self-esteem because you know that you helped someone else feel good. And in turn, you feel good all over again.

The friendlier you are and the bigger your smile, the more doors will open for you. It's not uplifting to be around people who are sad-sacks. We are, however, drawn to people who are happy and have a big smile on their face. The more people want to be around you, the more you will be thought of as a leader. And it all started with you being a leader of happiness.

Want to improve your self-image?

Change your posture. There are many benefits to standing up straight and having your chest out. They are both equally important. Proudly inflate that chest. Great posture not only enhances your emotional well-being, but also your physical well-being. Just the act of standing straight and tall enhances your self-esteem. Add a smile if you want to triple the effect. Try it now. You will feel the effect instantly.

Positive body language releases a healthy amount of endorphins, which is the body's natural morphine. It also enhances your breathing by making you take deeper breaths. This brings more oxygen, one of the body's natural healers, into your system. Dr. Andrew Weil believes that deep breathing is important. He recommends we take ten minutes a day to do some deep breathing techniques in order to add proper amounts of oxygen to our body.

Any time I notice myself slumping as I walk, I consciously push my chest out, and start walking tall—like I am walking with purpose. I notice that doing this instantly gives me an edge of feeling great. If I add a smile, I feel even better.

Want to improve your self-image?

Take a public speaking course. Get yourself in front of a group and express yourself. The ability to speak in front of an audience does so much to build your self-image and confidence.

Want to improve your self-image?

Visit someone who is homebound, or in a hospital or nursing home. Take a homeless child to a ballgame. Become a volunteer. Take a meal to a family in need. Whatever tugs at your heart, you can find someone with a need that fits what you are compassionate about. Don't do it just so others will admire you. Let it be your secret.

Make it a habit to look people in the eyes when you speak with them. This simple act will enhance your self-esteem in knowing that you have the confidence to make eye contact with another person—and smile. It is absolutely impossible to smile at someone, have him or her return the smile, and not feel good.

Also make a habit to compliment someone who does

something that impresses you, or thank them when they have done something nice for you. It's rare to pay somebody a compliment and not benefit yourself as a direct result.

I was having lunch at a Japanese restaurant in Arizona, and I mentioned to the waiter that I was really impressed with the quality of the fresh vegetables in their chicken teriyaki rice bowl. While dining, he brought me a coupon and said that I should use it on my next visit. He said he appreciated my business and asked that I, "Please come back again." The simple act of my compliment led to an interaction where I felt good, he felt good, and it made that moment exceptional. Beyond that, I made a new friend who will welcome me and make me feel special when I return to the restaurant in the future.

The first thing to do when you have made the decision to change your life is to stand up in front of the mirror and say out loud to yourself, "I am going to make great changes that are going to positively enhance my life."

I know that for most of you, doing this is going to be a little uncomfortable, but do it anyway. The best way to overcome a fear is to do some self-talk—coach yourself about what it is you are getting ready to do—and then **just do it**. Sometimes this is easier said than done, but if you practice this technique, you will become better at getting yourself to take action, and you will get more comfortable taking on new tasks. I recommend doing this every day for a month. By the end of the month it will be natural and you'll notice a distinct difference in your mindset.

Don't forget to have that big, beautiful smile on your face every time you do this, because the smile will enhance your emotion and make the effect even greater. You may smile anyway at first, because you feel somewhat "silly" standing in front of the mirror making the statement. But I promise that your world will change dramatically.

You will want to make some dramatic changes, so think creatively about the "new" you. Do some daydreaming. Change your hair-style or color, get your hair cut more often to keep yourself looking "fresh", dress up a little more, get a manicure and pedicure as a way of saying, "I am becoming different."

Assess your appearance. Could you benefit from losing weight or exercising? Do you have some tattoos that you've outgrown? Remove them. How about facial piercings, ear grommets, or counter-culture dress or hair? If you really want to advance in the business world, you might have to change some of these things, since most business cultures frown upon these styles. You'll like the new you, and it will help your self-image to know that you are taking better care of and investing in yourself.

Shine your shoes more often, buy a couple of new sets of clothes, and make a point of getting some things that are really nice. You don't need to get carried away, but *do* find some things that make you want to say, "I look great in this!"

In addition to the spending cash you normally have with you, start carrying at least one, if not two, $100 bills with you all the time. This creates the security of knowing that you always have money with you, and it will also give you, what I like to call, the **rich effect**. Subconsciously, you will feel more at ease and more comfortable knowing that you have cash with you "in case of an emergency."

I always carry a minimum of $1,000 in my wallet. If the

wad dwindles, I immediately get more, so I am always ready. Cash is more powerful in your wallet than in your savings account. But of course, you still need to save some money, so if you don't have a savings account, go open one and deposit ten percent of your earnings in it every payday. This may seem like a hard thing to do in today's economy, but remember, you have made a commitment to be different and these are the things that will lead you to a more positive self-image.

Spend time cleaning and straightening your house. Rearrange your furniture as another gesture to confirm that says, "I am changing my life." Wash and vacuum your car more often. All of these things will boost your pride. The prouder you are, the more self-confident you will become. The more self-esteem and the more enthusiasm you have, the more powerful you will feel everyday as you go out to change your world.

Do a few things that you may have always wanted to do, but didn't, because you never felt you had the guts, or because you didn't think you could overcome the obstacles. It doesn't have to be as dramatic as jumping out of a plane—unless that excites you. Something I always feared was being in the water. I almost drowned when I was younger, so this phobia remained with me. Being in a small boat, in the deep end of a pool, and definitely putting my head under water were always scary situations for me.

I decided one day that I had to overcome this fear because in many ways I really loved water. I got in a swimming pool, of course in the shallow end, took a deep breath, and put my head underwater for about fifteen seconds. It wasn't an overwhelming feat, just something small to start the process of overcoming that fear.

I did it several more times over the next few days, until it felt comfortable. Then I went to one side of the pool, still at the shallow end, put my head under the water, and swam underwater from one side of the pool to the other; again, nothing overwhelming, but more than I had done before. I kept doing this until the fear subsided. Then I swam from the shallow end of the pool to the deep end, and back to the shallow end, all the while underwater. I kept doing that until I was comfortable.

This may not seem like a big accomplishment to many, but for me it was. I am still cautious when I am in the deep end of a pool, but I am dramatically better than I used to be, and it has made a big difference for me in my self-confidence in the water.

Everything that you overcome gives you confidence to go out and do more. The more you do, the more you build your self-esteem. The more self-esteem you have, the happier you will be with yourself and with others.

Don't forget: ***I like myself, I love my life, I am excited, I am happy, I am healthy, and I add brightness to the life of everyone I meet.*** **Please repeat often.**

Psychologically it is impossible to watch mankind at its worst and not be affected. Avoid the daily soap opera or reality show. I have not seen more than two minutes of any of these in the last thirty years, because they are so negative. Real life just isn't that intense or extreme, but we have a tendency to find some way to identify with what we see. We see something on the screen, pick out a situation that in some minimal way reminds us of something in our life, and then make the irrational leap of identifying with that person or situation.

Did you know that two-thirds of medical students develop the symptoms of diseases they study? Medical students who study frightening diseases routinely imagine having the disease of the week—whatever they are studying.This temporary kind of hypochondria is so common, that it is called Medical Student Syndrome. **Don't fill your mind with things you don't want.**

Failures can teach us a great deal, if we let them. Hank Aaron struck out more times than any player in the majors, yet no one considers Hank Aaron a failure. On the contrary, he is a baseball legend. Babe Ruth wiffed a lot too, do we consider him a failure? Not at all.

Vince Lombardi lost a lot of football games, but he's considered one of the greatest coaches of all time and has the Super Bowl trophy named after him as a legacy to his excellence. All of these men experienced failure, but they learned that the only difference between success and failure is that the successful person keeps getting back up until they make it.

Anyone who tells you that they don't care what others think about them or their actions is a liar. Everyone has a certain level of pride. But if you truly have a good, healthy self-image, you won't be obsessed by what others think and it won't rule the majority of your thoughts and actions.

Once *you* accept yourself, it is no longer a matter of life and death for others to accept you. Once *you* like you, then it doesn't matter if others do or not. You will be welcomed wherever you go because you are an authentic person. You are secure within yourself. Once you accept yourself, then all your symptoms of negativity will disappear.

Some of us, when we don't like ourselves, seek unhealthy ways of dealing with it. Those who get involved with drugs and alcohol typically do not like themselves or the way they conduct their lives. They are seeking a change, in any form. Others think that, if they just have enough money, they will like themselves—and everyone else will like them too. They believe that if they are "comfortable" enough, all the "security" will make them happy. But one of the greatest secrets in the world is the joy we receive when we do things for others, rather than focusing on our own needs and wants.

The hope is that we all have some security and comforts in our life, but if we really want to have a true feeling of contentment, we need to learn the value and importance of helping others. I have found that one of the fastest ways of building a healthy self-image is to help someone who, in all likelihood, has no means of giving you anything in return. Whatever "cause" speaks to you, there is almost certainly an organization out there that will provide the opportunity for you to work for that cause.

We certainly can help by donating money, but an even better way to help is to "roll up our sleeves" and get involved with one of those causes. Donate some of your time to help and interact with the people. When we help others, and see their smiles and gratitude, it gives us such an overwhelming feeling of joy that it is hard for me to understand why we all don't do it more often—why it is such a great secret. *Do* find a cause that you're passionate about, but if the cause stirs such emotion that you find it difficult to be productive, then it is probably best to stay away from that particular charity. If you're not sure what charity you want to work with, do some research. Contributing to meaningful causes is something that will enhance your life ten-fold.

Most of us focus on what we have not accomplished in our lives. We think too much about what we need to get done today, or about the "stupid" driver we are following in traffic, instead of taking the time to appreciate what is great about our lives.

Though we may have been programmed to have this narrow mindset, as adults, it is our responsibility to work on changing this toxic mindset. This is so important that we should have time set aside each week that we dedicate to working on our self-esteem and self-confidence.

For years I traveled all over the country for my companies doing sales work. While I was on the road, I made time for listening to self-esteem and business building audiotapes. Over the course of the last thirty—plus years, I have listened to more than 50,000 hours of educational information.

We all spend a great deal of time in our cars, and that is a perfect time to listen to audio recordings. Watch educational videos on your iPad when you are on a plane trip. Remember, self-esteem and self-confidence are the cornerstones of happiness and success. They are worth changing some of your old habit patterns for.

One of the things that can ruin self-esteem is having unrealistic expectations. My dad always complained about what we didn't do—or what we should have done, rather than complimenting us on the good things we had done. Still, all of my brothers and sisters have grown up to accomplish a number of impressive things. We all did a number of worthwhile things as children as well, but we never heard our dad praise these feats. His negative attitude and constant berating devastated our self-esteem, even though he may thought otherwise.

Not everybody can be number one. Both of the teams that make it to the Super Bowl are the best in America, but one team has to lose. Do the losing team members feel bad about themselves for a whole year? They may feel bad for a day or two, but they pick themselves up, and go back to their training. They know they are part of a great team with tremendous talents. Rather than dwelling on the loss, they start working on the next season.

We need to learn not to let that kind of adversity affect us long term. We need to accept that we're not always going to come out on top. It is okay to make a mistake, to not prevail *that* time. A lot of things are won and lost in our mind, so by consciously choosing what you put into your mind and by controlling your mindset, you will have a much happier life.

There are certainly a number of things parents can do for kids to raise their self-esteem, but two actions take primacy. The first is to **listen**. The biggest complaint I hear from children and teenagers is that nobody listens to them; no one pays attention to them. There was a study done where they surveyed 160,000 kids in America and asked them what they wanted most. The top answer was that they wanted to be listened to and loved by someone—to be understood and cared about.

We have to spend time *really* listening to our children. We must take the time to be involved in their lives and communicate with them in a way that shows our concern and love. CNN's Anderson Cooper interviewed Steve Perry of "Perry's Principles." Perry spoke about a teacher who had just been given an award for having the most students attend college after completing a program she created. In fact, one hundred percent of those who graduated from her program went on to attend college. The teacher believed that the most damaging issue regarding children today was that their parents were not spending enough time with them; and their parents, and other adults in their lives, weren't listening to them.

This teacher had all her students involved with community projects, and she made sure that the whole "team" of parents, other significant adults, and the children participated. And she obviously got remarkable results using this strategy. She achieved this result in spite of the fact that her school was in a community where, prior to her becoming involved, the percentage of children who went on to college was far less than fifty percent. **It is amazing what you can accomplish, if you just have the right mental attitude.**

In most American homes, people sit in front of the TV or computer while they eat dinner. Even if the whole family eats in the house "together," they are off in their own rooms, rarely interacting with one another. What if we all sat at the dinner table and encouraged each of our children to talk about what was special for them in their day? And the parents could talk about their day as well. We might actually learn about what is happening in each other's lives and learn to diffuse potential bad behavior.

Every day of your child's life is time that you can spend making them feel important and teaching them all the important lessons of life. Sometimes as parents we become too focused on our own lives, and we don't take enough time to focus on helping our children learn to be good members of our community. Doing family activities that revolve around the community and helping others is a great lesson to teach our children. It's okay to take time for yourself, but you still need to meet the needs of your children. The important thing is to achieve balance.

The second action parents can take to raise their kids' self-esteem is to **praise** them. We need to encourage our kids to participate in whatever activity interests them, and praise them for their efforts and accomplishments.

As they take little steps, we need to boost them and encourage them to take that next, even bigger step. If they only clean half of their room, praise them for it. Let them enjoy their feeling of accomplishment. Wait a few moments before bringing up the other half of the room. If they don't get all A's on a report card, praise them for the grades they did achieve, and encourage them in a positive manner to do what it takes to improve in the future.

There is a mindset that says, "Catch someone doing something right." Start looking for the good things instead of the bad things. We all have been raised with the mindset to look at the negative rather than the positive, so we forget to consciously focus on the *good*. If parents listened to their children, looked for the good, and then complimented them on the accomplishments they have achieved, their children would grow to have a stronger self-image. They would see a dramatic difference in their behavior in a matter of months. **Your children need to be told that you love them and that you care about them**.

It is not *just* your children who need positive input. Everyone wants to be loved and acknowledged. Have you ever been at a party and noticed that while you were talking to someone, their eyes were darting all over the place? You probably felt, *Gee, I am not very interesting to this person. They must be looking around for someone more interesting*. If we give people solid eye contact and listen sincerely, and if we acknowledge them for what they do right, we will start to see miracles happen. We will see people brighten up and become motivated to do even more good things.

Another technique for building a healthy self-image is called **success recall**. You simply think of a success from your past, close your eyes, and see yourself reliving that success. Focus on the details of the success, to the point that you vividly see, clearly hear, and emotionally feel what you felt during that experience.

If you practice this technique faithfully, you will become proficient at it. You will get to the point that you see, hear, and feel just as you did during that time. Success recall brings your body the same sensations you had at that time, your biochemistry shifts, and you get a positive flood of emotion into your body. The experience will literally propel you into more success.

I urge you to do this on a regular basis and experience the power this brings, because your body cannot tell the difference between a real event and a vividly imagined event. Images are even more powerful than previously believed, so we must learn to control the images, or they will control us. Obviously you can create negative images in your mind as well, but it will most certainly be counter-productive. As I mentioned earlier, a large percentage of medical students start to experience some of the same symptoms of the disease that they are studying. That is how powerful this can be—for good or for bad.

The most powerful of all the psychological functions is **imagery**. Start imagining that good things are *always* going to happen. Imagine that you are *always* going to be accepted. You *are* going to get that job you applied for, and your business ideas *are* going to get funded.

Start imagining that you are going to be a success, and imagine yourself accomplishing the dreams that you have. Visualize yourself as though you have already achieved the goal. When you state the goal as if it has been achieved, not only will you feel good at that moment, but it will also kick your subconscious into gear and start you thinking about ways to produce those positive results. **Thinking about your dreams as if they have already happened draws creativity out of our subconscious and "turns it on."**

Whether you realize it or not, we visualize before we do anything. It is just the way the mind works. If you walk across the road, your mind visualizes it before you take action. Henry Ford wanted to build cars. He had a picture—an image—of what he wanted. As he worked toward that goal, he faced continual challenges, but he always found the solution. He never quit. He kept on visualizing until he got what he wanted.

If you want to do something in life, whether it is to instill a habit, such as smiling more often, or being more aggressive in business; or you want to attain certain material things; or have enough money to be able to donate to your favorite charity; you must visualize it before it happens. Keep this process churning, it will fuel your creative subconscious, and you will have the ideas to produce the result.

The reason most people fail to reach their potential is because they need to decide what they want, commit to it, visualize it, and take the steps necessary to get it. Imagine yourself so powerful that you cannot do anything that doesn't align with the image you have. **You cannot hold one image in your mind and do something that is opposite of that image; it is impossible**.

If your self-image is that of an overweight person, you won't be able to lose weight. I often tell people, *take a picture of yourself, cut off the part of the photo with your head, and paste it onto a picture of someone who has a body that is your ideal. Paste that photo on your refrigerator, so that it will be the image you focus on, rather than something you don't want.*

If you have visualized something in the past that limits you from doing something in the present, then you must consciously visualize that you *now* have the ability to do that very thing. Napoleon Hill states, "**What the mind of man can conceive and believe, it can achieve**."

Emotions and enthusiasm: Tony Robbins calls this "personal power." You must want what it is that you *say* you want, and you must have a great deal of passion for it. If you don't, you will never achieve it. This skill of personal power can be learned just like any other personal trait.

As you decide what you want to be passionate about, and you learn everything you can about that subject, the enthusiasm begins to swell within you. As your expertise increases, so does your confidence. The more knowledge you acquire, the more confidence you will have, and the more passionate you will become.

Positive feedback from others is a potent passion-builder. The more you get involved with your projects, the more others will take notice of your exciting progress.

If you are doing something positive, people will not only notice, but they will comment about what you are doing. Don't be afraid to politely ask for feedback at the infant stages of your project. I always welcome feedback, and it makes me smile when people compliment my work.

Another way to build enthusiasm, that is a game-changer, is to **daydream**. I am a daydreamer, and I encourage myself to daydream even bigger. When I daydream, I think through all of the possibilities and "what if's." One of the most powerful things you can do in your life is to spend one hour, three or four days a week, sitting in a totally dark room, letting your mind wander. You will be amazed at how many problems you will solve with this practice. I like to sit with a flashlight and a pen and paper, so I can write down all of the great thoughts that pour into my mind.

This practice is vital in building your enthusiasm, it gives you the feeling that you can do anything; and believing you can do *anything* powers your enthusiasm like a rocket. If you start this practice and continue it for the next forty years, you will be one of the "greats" who helps change the world. There is a great quote by Albert Einstein that I have framed and hanging in my house: "**Imagination is more important than knowledge.**" Thomas Edison said, "**If we all did the things we are capable of doing, we would literally astound**

ourselves." My request to you is to go out and daydream your way to happiness and success.

Another one of these very important choices, though not always as easy as it sounds, is to **do what you love**. Every successful, happy person will confirm that the main reason for their success is that they are doing what they love to do. Unfortunately, there is an old myth in our society that work is the penalty you pay during the day so that you can do what you enjoy during the evenings and weekends. Work is too often viewed as punishment. Because of this attitude, we don't do our jobs with as much dignity, and we refuse to discover ways to make our work challanging and enjoyable. If you are going to strive for true happiness, you have to change your attitude toward work.

Your life is too precious and valuable. Every minute of it should be spent doing things you love and care about. The wonderful reality is that the highest paid people are usually found working at jobs they love. The lowest paid people are often found at jobs they don't like, they are like robots going through the motions.

If you are in a job that you are not that excited about—and it shows, then how likely is it that your boss, noticing your lousy attitude, is going to give you a promotion? It is when you have a great attitude even when you are doing a job that is "not everyone's favorite," that the boss will say, "This person has shown a great attitude, even in *this* job, so they are definitely someone I want to keep on the team and advance."

Here are three habits that will propel you to greatness:

1) Invest three percent of your income back into yourself.

Spend that three percent on personal "research and development" and on upgrading your skills. If you invest three percent back into yourself, you will never have to worry about money again. Never become complacent about this, even as you begin to attain success. If you do, you will find yourself slipping backward.

2) Read for one hour each day in your chosen field. Take careful notes you can review regularly. Highlight important points, then go back and transfer all those points into a spiral notebook or an iPad. You will then have a synopsis of important ideas you can read until you memorize them. This method is used by some of the most successful people in the world.

3) Listen to CDs in your car. Turn your car into a "university on wheels." Always have educational and motivational CDs playing. You spend between five hundred and a thousand hours each year in your car. If you turn that driving time into learning time, you can become very well educated, certainly an expert in your field.

Invest in your education so that you can excel at everything you do. This continuous investment in yourself will put you behind the wheel of life. And by the **law of indirect effort,** this commitment to yourself will earn you the self-esteem, respect, and personal pride you desire. You will ultimately achieve the competence and mastery in your field. There is no limit to what you can accomplish if you know the direction you are going in, and if you are willing to make the effort.

Developing **internal integrity** is another building block

of a healthy self-image. Zig Ziglar says that "*What you do in the dark when no one else is looking is internal integrity.*"

When I was a young kid growing up in the Chicago area, we had a small neighborhood store right across the street from us. One day I strolled in, broke, but I craved a candy bar. I was young and foolish, so I took a candy bar, put it in my pocket, and walked out. I thought I was in the clear, but the lady who owned the store saw me take the candy. She told my brother, who then told my mother.

Of course I got in trouble. My mother told me why it was wrong to steal the candy bar, and she explained the potential consequences of doing things like this. I am sure I was sorry for what I did; however, I unfortunately can recall doing similar things at least a dozen more times over the next fifteen years. I justified it by saying that we were "so poor," and that what I stole was something I "needed." Somehow that helped me justify the thefts.

The last time I did anything like that was when I was about nineteen years old. I was in college and married for the first time. I felt like I needed a new pair of shoes because I wanted to look sharp for job interviews. I went to the local K-Mart, tried on a few, and found a pair I liked. My wife encouraged me to put them on and walk out without paying. It took some time to get the courage to do it, but then, like a dummy, I put the shoes on and walked out.

I didn't even get past the front sidewalk outside the store before the security guard stopped me and asked me about the shoes. K-Mart called the police, and they came and took me to jail. Sitting in the jail cell scared me to death. Fortunately, my brother-in-law came and bailed me out. I was so embarrassed that I just couldn't stand it, so I made the decision that I would never do something like that again. I could have gone the way of *more* crime and *less* achievement. Instead, by making a choice to change and "never go there again," I began the process of building more integrity. I changed my life and became a better person. Now I would never think about taking something that doesn't belong to me. If I am not charged for an item at the store, I bring it to the cashier's attention.

I try to show responsibility in other ways too. When I go to a movie theatre, I always take the empty popcorn bag to the garbage can, rather than leaving it for the attendants to pick up. Good members of society take responsibility. They don't expect others to pick up after them. Even though the attendant is paid to clean up the movie theatre, I know that it adds to the cost of the tickets for everyone when we don't pick up after ourselves, so I make the effort to do what I can. Just as good habits build a healthy self-image, taking responsibility for yourself enhances your self-esteem. Not taking advantage of others builds integrity and maintains your self-image.

Sometimes it makes sense to accept re-sponsibility, even when something is "not your fault." If you have a situation where you are partially to blame, or it is difficult to determine who is at fault, then be the bigger person, and accept the responsibility for it. Apologize, shoulder the blame, and get the situation resolved. You will feel good about yourself, and your self-esteem will be greatly enhanced as a result.

When you make a mistake, even one that is embarrassing to admit to, speak up and accept responsibility. Take care of it in a manner that shows how much integrity you have.

Set a standard for what is right for *you* and your self-comfort. Once you establish these standards, you can focus on what it takes to achieve your internal well-being. You will know the measure of what makes you feel good. You will find contentment and the satisfaction of real happiness.

Relationships and Success

Denis Waitley says, "A touch is worth a thousand words." Touch is the magic wand of intimacy and caring. When you touch someone, you triple the effect that you have, which is much more impactful than just telling someone that you care about him or her.

I grew up in a family where touching and hugging had a negative connotation. My parents had a bad relationship. If my dad would touch my mother, she would pull away and complain about him touching her. I grew up afraid to touch people, because I was conditioned to think that whomever I touched would complain and feel that I was being inappropriate. This is just one of the many reasons I became quite an introvert when it came to building relationships.

Not only did I have the same fear that most people with

a poor self-image have, the fear of being rejected, but I also assumed that no one *wanted* to be touched. I always thought of touching someone, no matter in what manner it was done, was inappropriate. That's all I ever witnessed growing up.

I have heard the statement that couples should stay together, even when they basically hate each other, "for the good of the children." But I question this belief. I had a massive struggle overcoming the negativity about relationships from watching my parents be very unkind to each other. It filled me full of negative ideas about how married couples interact. This is still one of my biggest challenges in life today.

It is devastating for children to watch their parents constantly battle, instead of seeing positive interaction and intimacy. Watching this kind of behavior inhibits a child's ability to handle intimacy in the future. They often find it difficult to hug and touch others as they reach adulthood.

I was listening to Brian Tracy thirty years ago talking about how touch was such a tremendous expression of affection, and that it dramatically multiplied the connection between people. He said that if you wanted another person to know how much you cared about them, you needed to add a "touch" as you verbally comforted them.

This way of thinking was profound to me. I had grown up associating touch with negativity. As I listened to that audiotape several times, I was determined to add this dimension of touch to my future communications. Just the thought of touching another person scared me to death; I was so afraid of invading another person's space. But with this newfound determination, I made the decision to make that first touch happen.

At the time, I had the manufacturing company that I mentioned earlier, so I had a significant number of people working for me. Although I told people on a regular basis that I really appreciated how hard they worked and the good job they did, I wanted to take things further by adding "touch" with my genuine statements.

I was around twenty-seven and had a female employee who was about forty-five working in the assembly area. She was a great employee who was always willing to work overtime when we needed a shipment to go out—which was often. I *did* tell her how much I appreciated her, but I knew that if I was going to follow Brian Tracy's advice, I needed to add that touch when I expressed my appreciation. Tracy said that in the case of an associate, friend, or employee relationship, a good way to touch someone is to use the tip of your hand, touching him or her on the top of their shoulder. He remarked that a pat on the back or the tip of their elbow would be appropriate, as this kind of touch would not be interpreted as threatening or sexual.

So one day, when we were busy and I knew she would be working overtime, I went to the female employee and began talking to her as she worked. I was so nervous that I could feel myself shaking. I talked to her for several minutes, and then I reached out and touched her on the top of her shoulder. I told her how much I appreciated her and the overtime she worked to help me get our orders out.

I was really excited about the fact that I was able to overcome my fear of touching her, and it was so gratifying to know that I had made the connection with her more impactful. The interaction put the biggest smile on my face. I knew she felt the connection too. She said that she was happy to be working for me, and that she appreciated the extra hours, as her husband's small business was slow and they really needed the money to help cover her family's financial shortfalls.

This was such a life-changing event for me. From that day forward, I became a huge toucher and hugger. I hugged and touched so many people that when I went to the local Chamber of Commerce meetings, everyone teased me that women would line up to give me a hug because I gave such good ones.

I make a point to reach out and touch men when I talk to them also. I pat them on the shoulder or touch their elbow as we talk. I would encourage you to learn to touch people when you interact with them, as long as you make sure to do it in an appropriate way. It has been so fulfilling to me. I don't know how I made it through life before I started doing it. In fact, if I go very long without hugging or touching someone, I go through "withdrawals."

There is, however, another aspect of touch that I want to address. For some people, touch has a negative connotation for a valid and unfortunate reason. They are resistant to their partner's touch. They equate being touched by that person with being threatened, because that person has a history of physically abusing them. This is why, as I mentioned previously, that my mother hated being touched by my father in any way. I certainly—and emphatically—encourage anyone in that type of situation to find a way out and leave!

Men love to touch, and for them, it is a sign of affection. If a woman dismisses a man's touch, she will drive a huge wedge between them. It can be a big enough wedge, such that if she continues to resist and complain about the touching, a man may start looking for someone else to fulfill his needs.

Men, listen carefully. You must learn the art of kindness and caring as you touch. Intimacy is a two way street and you don't have to be macho all the time.

Kindness, caring, intimacy, touching, communicating are all part of a successful relationship.

A good way to begin a relationship is to be an effective "physical" communicator. We offer friendliness to strangers by extending *our* hand first when greeting. This is a time-proven courtesy of initiating friendship to others. Along with a firm handshake, direct eye contact and a warm open smile show someone that you are interested in their company. Volunteer your own name first when meeting strangers, and start the conversation by saying, "Good morning," or "Good afternoon." This applies to phone conversations too. People can hear and feel a smile "through" the phone.

Once you introduce yourself, become an active and sincere listener. You begin to see that *listeners* learn a great deal, while *talkers* learn very little. You look forward to new contacts and friends. You talk easily with strangers and listen openly and caringly, even when you disagree with what they are saying.

You listen to each person from an equal frame of reference, since each person has his or her own story. You ask questions without imposing or interrupting. You try to find unique qualities in those you meet, and you praise people genuinely. You draw strangers out by trying to talk to them about themselves. You are understanding and easy to get along with.

You don't assume what the other party's reaction will

be, nor do you try to read his or her mind. You realize that many people harbor at least some fear of rejection or exploitation, but at the same time, you are enthusiastic when you greet strangers because you know that most everyone is eager to meet new people and gain friendship. When you interact with a potential friend, business prospect, or one of your own family members, your attitude is *service*-oriented, not *self*-oriented. Your concern is for the other person, not yourself. **When we have another's interest at heart, not just our own, they can sense it.**

Conversely, people get an uneasy feeling when they interact with those who have only *their* self-interest in mind. Their attitude comes across in their non-verbal communication. And like they say, "actions speak louder than words," so although someone's tongue may lie, their body will "speak" the truth. People can "hear" through the façade.

Many believe that we all have a "soul mate," or true love. The idea is that each person is born incomplete and is only truly happy when they find that "right" person with whom they can have a secure, lasting relationship.

Your ability to succeed in close, personal relationships affects your self-confidence in every other aspect of your life. Most young people in their twenties date a wide variety of people, as they discover what they really want in a relationship.

At the same time, they change jobs, spend everything they earn, and often move around from place to place. As they settle down into a more permanent relationship, their whole orientation changes. They make their decisions based on a "long term" point of view, rather than focusing on "instant gratification." They become more responsible, start to accumulate assets, and are more careful with their money. They begin to feel more connected with other people and with society. They have a greater sense of belonging to their community. As a result, their self-esteem improves.

The best relationships instill happiness and peace of mind. Everything you do that increases your ability to improve the quality of your relationship, also increases your self-confidence and self-esteem.

A good relationship gives you the strength and courage to take on challenges. Being *happily* involved with the right person clarifies your vision and encourages you to set loftier goals for yourself. It gives you a sense of inner security and added optimism, as well as a positive mental attitude toward everything you do.

The question arises that if everyone wants a healthy relationship, why is it that so few people, by their own admission, fail to achieve it. Why is it that so many people are alone, single, unhappy, or in marriages and relationships that are empty and unsatisfying? Why is it that people do not have the love that they want and need in their lives? What are some specific things that you can do to enhance the quality of your loving relationships?

Firstly, we must be very careful whom we choose as a mate. As part of the process of finding a mate suited for you, take the time to make a list of what is important to *you*, and try to find similar qualities in your potential mates. No one is going to be perfect for you, but we must give a great deal of thought and energy to picking that special person. When we are young, we are impatient, and as a result, we may jump into questionable relationships. Sometimes we let "chemistry" and hormones control us, and before we know it, we are married, only to find we don't have enough in common to keep us together for the long term. We should remember that our personal happiness is greatly entwined with our intimate relationships. If you are unhappy in your relationship, you will undoubtedly be an unhappy individual.

Commitment is an absolute necessity if we want to experience a deep-seated happiness in that one special relationship. But no matter how committed *you* are to the relationship, if your mate walks out—emotionally or literally—you can't force them to stay. If you are in a relationship with someone who has a poor self-image, you can't force them to be happy with themselves. And though it is important to value the commitment, there can unfortunately come a time when a relationship needs to end.

I don't believe in being committed to misery in any area of life. We only have one life to live, and it is far too short. We don't need to punish ourselves—or the other person—forever, because we made a mistake in choosing our mate, or because one—or both—have changed. People *do* change. What they allow to influence them is out of your control. You must be absolutely committed if you expect to have true happiness, but you also must be able to see and acknowledge a one-sided commitment.

We should strive to share ourselves out of choice, as an independent person, not lose ourselves in a co-dependent relationship. True love is that relationship formed by two individuals who have the ability to separately sustain themselves. Only independent people are free to choose to stay in a relationship. People who are dependent remain in a relationship out of necessity.

We have become a more narcissistic society, motivated by the desire for immediate gratification. So many people are unable to express themselves in spontaneous, intimate communication. They have become skilled technicians in the sexual act, yet they are afraid to expose themselves to the vulnerability inherent in intimacy. Our intimate relationships suffer under the media hype, which promotes performance over closeness and commitment. While sex is everywhere, intimacy has seemed to all but disappear.

Ironically enough, the secret to intimacy is not hard to learn. Not a morning should go by in your relationship that the opening minutes of the day are not devoted to mutually satisfying words and actions. After the day's activities are completed, make it a point to devote the first couple of minutes to each other.

Never greet each other with a pressing question or complaint. Don't forget to touch each other and relax soon after you get home. Surprise your mate with a card of remembrance. If you are the one being surprised, make sure you show enthusiasm and gratitude for that surprise. Pretend you are still dating and always look forward to seeing your loved one. If you really want to be loved in life, you must first be lovable. There is no such thing as "love on demand," or "you promised me ten years ago you'd love me forever." Love is a daily, mutual exchange of values. Nothing transmits value so clearly, however, as the physical touch. Use your sense of touch generously. If you are not following this message of mutual exchange, the relationship with fall apart or be empty.

The most precious moments you will ever spend with your children are those moments just before they go to sleep at night. Many activities are going on in the typical family every day: dinner, homework, chores, video games, finances, etc. There is little wonder that the average American parent spends less than seven minutes each week alone with each child, one on one, at a time when each one is receptive. This is so prevalent that our relationship with our children has been referred to as a "Seven-Minute Per Week Syndrome." Children spend more time with the TV, their phones, or their computers, than they do communicating with their parents.

The **law of correspondence** states that your outer world is a mirror of your inner world. Your relationships mirror the kind the kind of person you are. These relationships include all your thoughts, attitudes, fears, and desires. They are a measure of you as a person. Most of what you see in your relationships, including your marriage, is actually a manifestation of your interior world. This is why it is almost impossible to have a healthy relationship or marriage if you don't have a healthy self-image.

Whenever you are having difficulty in your relationships, you should ask, "What is it in me that is causing this other person to behave this way?" Or, you can ask, "What is it in me that is causing this relationship to manifest in this way?" As you change what is going on inside yourself, you will see the same changes take place in the people around you.

By changing yourself, you change them. By becoming a better person, your relationships get better. By becoming more patient and happy, your relationships become more relaxed, happier and loving. Truly loving people have little difficulty forming loving relationships.

The **law of attraction** says that you are a living magnet, and that you attract people and circumstances that are in harmony with your dominant thoughts. People are attracted to you because of the kind of person you are. You can change the people around you by changing the kind of person you are. As you work to change yourself, by dwelling on your positive qualities, you immediately change the force field of energy around you. As a result, you begin drawing into your life people who are more like your new ideals.

The great mistake most people make is that they try to change others into the person they want *them* to be, rather than going to work to change themselves. However, when you think honestly about how hard it is to change the smallest thing in yourself, you will realize the futility you will encounter in trying to change someone else. The same skills that are required to be successful in your casual relationships apply with equal force to your marriage, or your other special relationships. If you want to be happy with that "special" person, become the kind of happy person that he or she would like to be around. Be pleasant and agreeable. Be cheerful and supportive. Make the other person feel important by validating and reinforcing their self-worth.

Above all, be a good listener. Each person has a deep need to communicate their inner-most thoughts and concerns to another person; and they are invariably attracted to the person who will listen most intently, and honestly. Many have found that paying close attention to what someone is saying is the highest form of flattery. Listening—and that means both of you—builds trust and intimacy.

The ability to communicate well is a requirement for happiness between two people.

Each person has a deep need to express himself or herself to another person. A person wants to be heard without judgment or interruption. If we don't get a chance to get all of our "talking" out of our systems, it bottles up inside, and we become frustrated. The start to most problems in a relationship is the result of failing to keep the line of communication open.

The quality of commitment perhaps more than any other, ensures effective communication and guarantees a happy relationship.

Successful couples are those who are totally committed to each other. They see the other person as their best friend. When two people are in the right relationship, they enjoy each other's company so much that there is no one else with whom they would rather spend their time. They each feel themselves to be half of a whole, incomplete without each other, and totally committed to being together forever. Commitment without reservation is an absolute requirement for happiness in a relationship. While commitment does not guarantee complete success in a relationship, a lack of commitment will almost certainly guarantee failure.

People "telegraph" their expressions and feelings without even realizing they are doing it. The listener "hears" the whole person, both what they are verbalizing, as well as what they are physically communicating. Successful communicators know that each of us sees and hears in our own unique way. Because we tend to *get back* from people what we *give* them, it is best to communicate using simple, productive, supportive ideas. If we want to be loved, we need to communicate positive, loveable language.

You can only communicate honestly when you are sure that the other person has closed the door to his or her old relationships and has made a complete commitment to you and this relationship. Charles Murray, a noted author and mountain climber, once wrote, "Until one is committed, there is hesitancy."

If commitment is the key to a happy, love relationship, then why is it that so many people have such a difficult time making this commitment? The answer brings us back to self-confidence and self-esteem. You can only like or love another person to the degree which you like or love yourself.

An excellent relationship or marriage is essential to the development of a healthy personality. To the extent that you are secure with another person, you can relax and tell the person what is going on deep in your mind without fear of rejection or criticism. It is only then that you understand the full depth of your personality.

In psychology, it is believed that often when a person is unhappy, it is because of some underlying issue that needs to be addressed. As soon as the person can honestly discuss this problem, they begin to free themselves from the shackles of the problem. Meaningful and relevant self-disclosure leads to higher levels of self-awareness. The more of yourself that you can *honestly* disclose to another person, the more you become self-aware. Instead of repressing your true thoughts and feelings, you can release them and discover more of who you are and what possibilities exist for you.

As you find yourself truly enjoying the company of other people, the quality of your loving relationships dramatically improves. No one ever finds real happiness from self-serving activities and thoughts. It is only when you focus on the needs of others that you become truly happy.

Don't forget: ***I like myself, I love my life, I am excited, I am happy, I am healthy, and I add brightness to the life of everyone I meet.*** **Please repeat often.**

As you take full control of your mind and keep your words and thoughts consistent with the very best person you can be, you triggera all the positive mental laws and create a tremendous feeling of well-being that generates a steady flow of energy and self-confidence.

As you become more capable of getting along with a wider variety of people, your confidence and your ability to interact effectively in all your human relations goes up, and you become fearless in new situations. Every step of the way, as you apply these lessons, you are building yourself, brick by brick, into the kind of person you really want to be.

Now let's talk about some of the differences between men and women, and how some of these differences lead to misunderstandings and breakdowns in the communication. First of all, men and women are distinctly different from one another. In the material world, they may have similar goals and objectives; but in the personal, subjective world, they have distinctly different motivations, desires, instincts, and ways of looking at life and relationships. Some of the differences are obvious and some are not. In order to survive and thrive with members of the opposite sex, it is helpful for us to appreciate some of the differences.

Men have a tendency to be more direct, more practical, and more left-brained in their thinking. They have more of the hormone testosterone, and as a result, they tend to be more aggressive in all aspects of life.

Men tend to be more competitive and job-oriented, continually comparing their achievements to those of other men. Men tend to identify strongly with their work, and they derive much of their self-concept from their occupations. The extreme version, of course, is called the Type A Personality.

The Type A Personality is so obsessed with work that very little else interests him. He feels like he is on a treadmill, or in a rat race. He has a sense of urgency and always feels that he has more and more to do and less and less time to do it. He seldom, if ever, takes a vacation; and if he does, he takes his work with him. He is extremely aggressive and hostile with those he feels he competes against, even those who are family; if they want more of his time than he feels he can spare.

He has an obsession with his boss, and often talks about what the boss did and said, and what he might be thinking. This extreme-minded person becomes more things-oriented as opposed to people-oriented, and he begins to take his personal and family relationships for granted. He has a compulsive, negative habit pattern, which is rooted in a deep fear of rejection and a feeling of unworthiness that relates to having experienced *conditional* love from his father. He craves approval from his boss and his work, which he feels he never got *unconditionally* from his father.

The Type A's pre-occupation with work becomes a major flashpoint at home, because it does not seem reasonable to his wife. He often says that he is doing it all for the sake of his wife and children, but they disagree and wish that he worked less and spent more time with them.

Men, in general, are very much into closure, a satisfied completion. A hazy outcome is very stressful. They are most interested in discussing situations that have clear conclusions and resolutions. Conversations are also geared toward specific goals and conclusions. Men have a tendency to be simple, direct, and largely uncomplicated in their thinking. They tend to think and talk in terms of facts and conclusions.

Any woman reading this will immediately recognize that her way of thinking is very different. Women have a much richer, more complex, and more interesting inner life. They are aware of far more details and subtleties than men. They see more possibilities, ramifications, and consequences in situations. If men tend to be direct, women tend to be indirect. Women are more subtle and roundabout in their approach to people and situations. If a woman is having a problem with someone, she thinks of the various ways of how the subject could be approached, so as to win the cooperation of the other person and not make waves or create confrontation.

A man in the same situation would tend to deal with a problem more directly. Either approach could be successful, but the evidence shows that women are more successful in dealing with complex, interpersonal relations. Women are more emotional, intuitive, sensitive, and more aware of what other people are thinking and feeling than are men. Women tend to organize their lives around their relationships with their family and friends. They are much more sensitive to—and affected by—problems in relationships than are men.

Here's a humorous example of the differences in the sexes. A husband and wife fly to Phoenix and rent a car, with the intention of driving south to Tucson. They get on the freeway and she is the navigator, looking at the map and road signs. He is unfamiliar with the roads. Suddenly the wife sees a sign that indicates they are heading north toward Flagstaff.

She asks him, "Is Flagstaff on the way to Tucson?"

He says, "No, Flagstaff is in the opposite direction."

She says, "Well, we just passed a sign that said we are headed toward Flagstaff."

"Never mind," he says, "we're making great time."

While the woman stops to think about where she is, and where she wants to go, the man just wants to step on the gas and reach his destination, even if it is the wrong one.

Another example is when a man and woman go shopping together. All he wants to do is get it over with before the walls close in around him. She, on the other hand, sees shopping as an opportunity to communicate. When she shows him a dress and asks for his opinion, she is inviting dialogue. He says, "It looks great. Go ahead and get it."

After a couple of hours of shopping, a woman may not have bought anything. By this time, he will be tearing his hair out and will suggest they go have coffee or lunch. He is looking for closure or completion. Until the shopping trip is over, the typical man will be uncomfortable. The difference: Men are simple, direct, and want closure. Women are complex, subtle, and quite content to simply enjoy the process.

Here's another example. A couple is three hours into a road trip. While driving, they pass by a McDonalds. The woman asks, "Honey, are you thirsty?" Without looking around, he says, "Nope," and continues driving.

After a while he notices the silence and when he asks, "What's the matter?" She replies, "Nothing." What happened in this scenario was that the woman was thirsty, and in her indirect way, suggested that they stop. In his direct way, the man simply replied to her question and continued driving. His mind was focused on the destination—on completing the trip—and he was unaware that she wanted to stop. And by the way, when a man does ask, "What's the matter?" and the woman replies, "Nothing," it is a very clear sign that something is the matter. If the man is smart, he will pick up on this signal and inquire further.

Because women are indirect, they tend to be better listeners and more sensitive to relationships than men. According to Cosmopolitan magazine, men are ninety-four percent more likely to interrupt a woman than a woman is to interrupt a man. When a man interrupts a woman, he is making a big mistake. Not only is he telling her that he doesn't take her seriously, he is also devaluing her as a person. By not allowing her to finish, he is unwittingly attacking her self-respect; and, we know whenever our self-respect is assaulted in anyway, we have a tendency to counter-attack. We often become angry and defensive, striking back in any way we can.

This is also true of the woman who interrupts a man. Common courtesy would suggest that we should spend more time listening than getting our point across.

The **law of reciprocity** governs almost all relationships. The law of reciprocity says that we should try to repay, in kind, what another person has provided us. For men, one of the ways to keep the channels of communication clear is to come home at night and resist the temptation to tell her everything about *your* day. Instead, you should ask her about *her* day. Ask her what she did, where she went, and who she spoke to during her day. This simple exercise of turning the standard tables of conversation will go a long way toward enhancing your relationship.

Here is another common occurrence which shows the quality of a relationship. When the woman tells her other half about a problem she is having at work, he immediately goes into problem solving and closure mode. He asks her a few questions, and then he bombards her with suggestions.

What he doesn't realize is that she doesn't necessarily want him to propose a solution at all. Discussing the problem is merely an opportunity to talk and vent. She has presented the problem as a device to trigger a dialogue. If he gives her a quick solution, she will feel frustrated, and he won't even know what has happened. **Two of the most valuable tools a man can use to enhance a relationship are listening and asking questions**.

The best thing that a woman can do is realize that men deal with things differently than women. She must take this into consideration. Remember, the most important thing in the world is **love**. First self-love, then love of others, and then love of that one person with whom you can establish a deep and lasting relationship. Out of loving and being loved arises a wonderful feeling of self-confidence that gives you the courage to attempt things you never thought were possible. Knowing that you are truly loved, and that you have earned and deserve it, saves you an enormous amount of energy. It also allows you to focus on making your life a wonderful experience.

Eighty-five percent of your success in life will depend upon the quality and quanity of your relationships. In every society and every organization, the person who knows the greatest number people—and is known to them in a favorable way—is almost always the person with the greatest power and influence. Dr. Abraham Maslow was an American professor of psychology most known for his concept of a "Hierarchy of Needs." Maslow suggested that the need for affiliation, to be liked and accepted with a work or social group, is indispensable to your mental health.

Most of us learn relationship skills from the manner in which we grow up, and we tend to "stick with what we know." The relationship skills that I learned growing up were quite weak. I knew that I needed to "retrain" myself and learn more valuable and refined skills than what I "experienced". In many instances, parents have spent little time with their children, and as a result, their children learn much of their social and relationship skills from TV or other outside influences. As they reach adulthood, hopefully those children will take the time to educate themselves on how to improve those skills, just as I did.

These skills, however, are indispensable to your self-confidence. They satisfy your ego and social needs, and they

are closely linked with physical well-being and longevity. According to the experts, people with weak social ties are three times more likely to die prematurely then those with strong social ties. Divorced men die from heart disease, cancer, and strokes at double the rate of married men. The rate of all types of cancer is as much as five times more for divorced men and women, compared to their counterparts.

The law of indirect effort applies to relationships very effectively. You get what you want from people through indirect means rather than direct means. When you become a relationship "expert," it will be because you are not thinking about yourself at all.

You will feel at your best when you are being yourself and you let the other person's personality shine through without attempting to shade it or change it in any way. You are more spontaneous, relaxed, humorous, and enjoyable to be around. You can never be more, or less, or different from the person you really are. Most people try to be something that they are not, and even worse, all in the guise of trying to be something to please the other person. When you practice the law of concentration and focus on your values and goals, these thoughts soak deep into your subconscious and cause you to act in a manner consistent with them.

Your job is to work on your inner world and let the outer world take care of itself. For example, if you have a problem with your child, an employee, or co-worker, always turn within and accept responsibility for triggering the behavior, whatever it is. It may turn out that the way the person is acting has nothing to do with you, but by holding yourself accountable, you take full responsibility and control and keep calm and focused.

One of the most important tools is the **law of reciprocity**. This law is based on the age-old axiom that whenever you do something for someone else, he or she feels a sense of obligation to you and can only remove that feeling by doing something of an equal or greater value for you. It also happens that if you do something unkind to another person, he or she will also have a tendency to reciprocate in kind.

The law explains why happy, self-confident people make more progress in five years than the average person may make in twenty years with equally hard work, sometimes even in the same company. Happy, self-confident people seek out every opportunity to do things for other people in advance. Over time, they build up a reservoir of good will and favors that cause people to want to help them get ahead. It's another example of sowing and reaping—cause and effect.

The more of yourself you give away to others with no direct expectation of return, the more you will receive back—sometimes from some of the most unexpected sources. The winner in life is the person who is always looking for opportunities to give. The loser is the one who is always asking, "What's in it for me?" When you are younger, you usually have more time than money, so you give your time. When you get older and you become more financially secure, you have less time, but more money, so you give financially. But the rule is to give whenever, whatever, and wherever you can, knowing that it will come back to you in abundance.

In your relationships, the same rule holds true. In every relationship, you want to make the other person feel important when they speak to you. When you do this, you raise their self-esteem, and in turn, you raise yourself-esteem. When you say and do things that cause people to like themselves and feel more confident, you like yourself more and you feel more confident about yourself. Dale Carnegie wrote, **"You can make more friends in two months by becoming really interested in other people than you can in two years by trying to get other people interested in you."**

Most everyone can improve their self-esteem. We all desire to be more valuable and important to others and to have our self-image reinforced. If you will deliberately give people what they want and need, they will reciprocate by giving you friendship, and you will be welcomed wherever you go.

I have five key actions you can take to build fulfilling relationships.

The first key is to be **agreeable**. Be amiable and open, be cheerful and positive, rather than argumentative and difficult. Make a habit of empathizing in all encounters, even conflicting ones. If you disagree and you feel you must say something, protect the self-esteem of the other person, by using Benjamin Franklin's method of stating your opinion in a very mild way. Don't tell a person that he or she is wrong or misinformed. Instead say, "I could be wrong, but I thought it was this way?" By doing this, you show that you are open and willing to change your mind and are flexible, rather than fixed in your ideas. People will enjoy being around you more, and will enjoy discussing different issues with you.

The second key is the practice of **acceptance**. Each person, from infancy, forms their self-image from the way that others react to them. Your children and your employees are greatly affected by the way you treat them. If you treat people as valuable and important, they think of themselves that way. They respond warmly and positively to you. When two people meet, especially for the first time, a certain level of acceptance is established—or not established—between them. Most obnoxious behavior is a cry for help. It is a cry to be accepted and liked by others.

One of the most powerful gestures you can do to help others feel comfortable in your presence is to look them in the eyes and smile. With warm, genuine eye contact, the other person feels important, knowing that you are interested in what they have to say.Their self-image improves and their self-esteem goes up. Because they feel good about themselves, in return, they feel good about you. And all it cost was a simple smile.

The third key is **appreciation**. When you show gratitude toward anyone, they feel more important and valuable. The key to expressing your appreciation is simply saying, "Thank you." I have traveled in many countries throughout the world, and the first phrase I learned in each country was *Thank You*. If you are polite, you very seldom have issues anywhere. People will open their doors and hearts to you. Opportunities abound that simply would not be offered to a person who was rude or demanding.

A wonderful way to raise your self-esteem is to develop an **attitude of gratitude**. Develop the habit of being thankful for everything. An attitude of gratitude enriches abundantly. I believe that being grateful is one of the core foundations of being truly happy. I have spent a number of years wishing and waiting to achieve that next goal in my life, forgetting to live in the moment with gratitude for everything that I had.

It took me a long time to learn it, but once I did, I started thinking of a way to anchor myself to this mindset. I was driving down the road one evening coming home from a seminar where I was the speaker. I was daydreaming when an idea hit me like a lightning bolt. I would design a "**Gratitude Coin**," and I would carry it with me in my pocket everywhere I went. Having the coin with me would remind me to be more grateful. I thought, *I want to make a coin for me, but I also want to find a company that will mass produce the coin. That way I can give them to everyone I meet who does something for which I am grateful, and I can tell them the meaning of gratitude as I give them the coin.* I could give the coin to people which would touch their lives in a positive way and it would supply the reminder for them remember to be grateful—just as it was going to do for me.

I pulled off the road, pulled out my note pad that I always carry, and I immediately designed the coin. On one side of the coin, it says in large letters "**GRATITUDE COIN**." The other side of the coin reads, "**I am grateful for…**" *What am I grateful for?* is a question that each of us should answer every day as we look at the coin. I always carry several of the coins in my pocket to hand-out, because I love the feeling I get when I give it out to strangers.

When I go to a restaurant, or a retail store, or wherever, and someone does something nice for me, I reflect on his or her kindness to me. If they have a smile on their face and are friendly as they take care of me, I give them a Gratitude Coin, and I tell them about its significance to me.

I'll say:

I wanted to let you know that I am grateful for your help, but I also want you to know that I believe that gratitude is the foundation of happiness and success. I believe that we don't remember to be grateful as much as we should, but I also believe that if you carry this coin with you and look at it every day, it will help you remember to be more grateful for everything you have, and you will be a happier person for the rest of your life.

People love the coin. It always puts a smile on their face, and of course, *that* puts a smile on my face. It has been, and continues to be, a wonderful experience for me to give these coins away and touch people's lives. It's awesome!

I was in *Home Depot* a few months ago, and as I reached in my pocket to pay for my purchase, the clerk asked, "What are those coins?"

I said," They are Gratitude Coins."

She said, "Oh, yes, you gave me one about six months ago, and I have it right here in my apron." She pulled it out, showed it to me, and smiled.

I also was at a restaurant not long ago that I had been to a couple of times before. As I was paying the server for the bill, I handed her a Gratitude Coin and explained it's significance.

She said, "I have one of these. My boyfriend works here as a server, and he got one a couple of months ago. He showed it to me, and I liked it so much that I took it from him so I could carry it."

I gave the waitress a couple more coins and said, "Give one to your boyfriend, so he can carry a coin too. And here's an extra one, so you can share your gratitude with someone else." Her face glowed as she thanked me.

I was at a restaurant in Nashville a few months for a meeting. Our meeting ran longer than expected, we took up the server's table for a couple of hours. I made sure I gave her a larger tip, and I thanked her for allowing us to stay at her table so long. As I squared the bill, I also handed her a Gratitude Coin and told her my story of wanting to express my gratitude for her smile and helpfulness.

As I finished, a tear started to roll down her cheek and she said, "You don't know what this means to me. I am in Alcoholics Anonymous right now, and we are learning the value of gratitude. I do feel grateful for the change in my life, and I will always carry this coin with me."

What a feeling it is to know that you are touching people's lives enough that months later they are still carrying the coin with them and thinking of being grateful. It has been as big a gift for *me* as it has been for them. Gratefulness. Pass it on. It will warm your heart over and over again.

A fourth key to improving your relationship with others is to practice **admiration** at every chance. Abraham Lincoln once said, "Everybody likes a compliment." Always be sincere when giving a compliment. People most appreciate it when you admire their character traits, their accomplishments, and their material possessions.

We each invest a large amount of our emotions in these things, and when we are admired and respected by another, our own sense of value and importance grows immediately. If you admire someone's work ethic, their punctuality, not only will people strive to repeat those behaviors, but they will also feel wonderful about themselves and appreciate that you noticed it. **The more emotion a person has invested into something, the more powerful and significant your compliment.**

When you admire specific articles of clothing, for example, they will often remember your remarks for years. Not always, but most of the time, when you notice a woman's shoes, she will smile for the rest of the conversation. Always be sincere. Never say anything that you don't mean. People are like human lie detectors. The average person can sense insincerity from across the room. If you say something you don't really believe, you will hinder your chances of building a positive relationship. Always be truthful, and always speak from your heart.

The fifth key is to practice giving **praise** wherever you go, you will find them everywhere. All you have to do is get yourself in the habit of *noticing* and the opportunity will present itself.

Praise people for both small and great accomplishments. Ken Blanchard, author of *The One Minute Manager*, stressed the importance of "one minute praising." He recognized that one of the best things a manager or parent could do was, as I mentioned earlier, to "catch someone doing something right." The more you praise and approve specific behaviors, the more likely it is that those behaviors will be repeated.

If you want to stop a person from engaging in negative behavior, simply ignore it. If you ignore negative behavior, yet also praise people for positive behavior at every occasion, eventually they will do more and more positive things for which they get praised and have less time for negative behavior.

Any praise coming from someone we respect has an inordinate impact on our self-esteem. This form of recognition is a great people-builder in organizations and a wonderful way to make and deepen relationships in your personal life. The Emperor Napoleon was famous for the way he motivated his armies to conquer all of Europe. When he was asked his secret, he said he learned a remarkable thing: "Men…will die for ribbons."

Here are four vital points about praise.

1) Praise immediately. The sooner you praise, the more likely it is to be repeated. Praise can be both tangible and intangible. It can be expressed in words or in rewards that you give. The closer the connection between the praise and the performance, the bigger impact it will have on the personality and future behavior of the person receiving the praise.

2) Praise specifically. Rather than say, "You are doing a really great job," say, "You did a terrific report for the meeting yesterday." Rather than say to your child, "You are a great kid." It's better to say, "You did a great job cleaning your room."

3) Praise in public whenever possible. Praise given in front of others multiplies the impact. Recognition and rewards given in front of the entire company will have a major influence on future behaviors. The more ceremony you can attach to the praise, the more motivated everyone will be to engage in the same performance in the future. Companies that recognize their employees each year at awards banquets build upon that foundation annually.

4) Praise continuously to develop the habit. You praise continuously by mentioning the behavior and complimenting the individual every single time it occurs. If you praise a person over and over, they will continue the behavior until it becomes a habit for them.

Can you remember a time in your life when you were totally in sync with another person? I had a couple of employees whom I shared this connection. It seemed that every time one of them would talk, the other would finish their sentence for them. Often, we would have a meeting and discuss a subject, and they would both bring up—and start talking about—the same detail at the same time. I don't believe I have ever heard anyone talk as fast as the two of them talked—and they could actually understand each other. I would regularly have to ask them to slow down, so I could hear and understand them. They had such rapport, it seemed as if they were twins.

We all experience this connection—this rapport—at some level with a variety of people in our lives. What is *rapport*? How is it created? How can we use it in our lives to produce more effective results? I am sure there have been times when you have tried to communicate with someone and there was just no feedback or connection. Or you have had a conversation with a new acquaintance, and suddenly something clicked and you connected like you had known them a long time. That connection—that shift—is what rapport is all about.

No one achieves massive goals unless they are able to

enlist a great deal of talented people to aid them. The best way to enlist the help of a strong team is for you to master the art of building rapport.

How does the average person build rapport? When we start a conversation, most people try to find something in common. We might say, "I live in Scottsdale, Arizona. Where do you live?"

Your acquaintance replies, "I used to live in Tempe, and I attended ASU."

"Oh, no kidding? Did you ever go to Tempe Marketplace and eat at Lucille's Smokehouse BBQ?"

"Sure. Isn't that a great place to eat?"

This conversation establishes a commonality, and it is the foundation for rapport. Commonality means people share a *common* bond—when people are *like* each other, they tend to *like* each other. That is what links people together. When you find that common bond, suddenly there is a new level of energy in the conversation and connection. Think of someone that you really like and ponder, *Is this person like me*? I'll bet they are. That is commonality—that sense of connection.

Conversation is the most common way most to start building rapport, but there is so much more to building intense rapport than just what is said. How many times have you noticed, as you are speaking to someone, that a person crosses *their* arms, then almost immediately, you cross *your* arms, almost like you followed their suggestive movement?

Or when you and a friend are talking, and they lower their voice to tell you a secret? Just the change in the volume and tone of their voice started to build excitement. This is all part of communication, and many believe that this form of communication is much more effective than the actual spoken words. Using your body language, the tone and volume of your voice, and changing the pace at which you speak are all very effective ways to build positive or negative excitement.

What about the way you use your eyes to communicate? Has there ever been a time when you were speaking to someone, and it seemed as if their eyes were on fire with excitement or despair? There is an old saying, "*The eyes are the windows to the soul.*" If you watch someone's eyes, they will tell you stories that you can't hear by just listening to their voice.

Read this section over again and daydream about how you can use these mechanisms to build rapport—to improve your level of communication, and ultimately enhance your relationship with others. The enhanced richness in your life will be worth every ounce of effort it takes to learn the lessons of building better relationships.

As my mother always said, "*Practice makes perfect.*"

Anchoring Yourself to Success

There are people who get goosebumps every time they see an American flag. It's an odd reaction, when you think of it. Analytically, it is just a piece of cloth. There is nothing inherently magical.

When it comes to the American flag, although it may be "just piece of cloth," it has come to stand for all the virtues and characteristics of the United States of America. The American flag is a powerful symbol that represents all the principles for which America stands. It is an anchor that has been linked to a specific set of emotions and state of mind. An anchor can be a word, phrase, touch, or object—and can be something you see, hear, taste, or smell.

Another word for anchor is "trigger." Anchors are the triggers to various, personal states of mind. When you see the

American flag, it triggers your emotions.

Our world is full of anchors. Some are profound and some are trivial. If you hear, "It's not just smart, …," your likely response is, "It's K-Mart smart." If you hear the song, "I've Had the Time of My Life," sung by Jennifer Warnes and Bill Medley, most think of the movie, *Dirty Dancing*, or possibly the frequently-played commercial for Sandals Resorts. These are anchors. The advertising has been so effective, the song or statement heard so frequently, that it creates a response in you—even when you're not actually watching the movie or commercial.

The same sort of stimulus-response occurs daily in our lives. We live in a **stimulus-response** world. When some people receive a *stimulus* that causes stress, they automatically reach for a conditioned *response*—food, cigarettes, or something to drink. Or you may run into a certain person, and instantly your state of mind changes—sometimes for the good, and sometimes for the bad. You can hear a song and have an instantaneous change in your mood. All these responses are results of powerful anchors.

Anchors are a way to give something permanence. We have learned how to change our state of mind by changing what we represent to ourselves and how we use our bodies. In order to create long-term change, we need to create a new anchor that changes our state of mind and gets us to take a different action. We need to create a triggering thought or action that will automatically cause us to change our state of mind.

If you do something effectively enough, it will provide that anchor whenever needed. The same response happens every time you use it. There are three different forms of anchors: **voice/**

sound, **vision,** and **touch**. There are certain songs that, when we hear them (*voice*), change our state of mind and emotions. You hear a love song that was playing on your first date with someone you love, and it reminds you of him or her and that time in your life. You see (*vision*) the Mickey Mouse icon, and you think of Disneyland. When someone you care about deeply comes up and puts their arm around you (*touch*), you feel loved.

We all *anchor* regularly. In fact, it's impossible not to. It is just a created association of thoughts and feelings with a specific stimulus. As an example, I have worked out of my home for many years. I built it with 1,700 square feet of office space on the top floor. For a long time, until she passed away, my mother-in-law fixed lunch for everyone in the office. She had a little bell that she had gotten from her mother. My mother-in-law would ring that bell every day when she had lunch ready for us, so we would know to come down and eat.

We all got so conditioned to that bell, that as soon as we heard it ring, we all would say, "Oh good, lunch is ready. I'm starving," whether we were hungry before the bell rang or not.

Much of human behavior consists of programmed, unconscious responses that come from our subconscious. For example, many people under stress reach for cigarettes or alcohol. They don't think about it, they just do it. Many of these people would like to change those behaviors, but they are unconscious reactions, so they just react automatically. The key to creating change is to become conscious of the process, so that the anchors can be replaced with new stimulus-responses, which in turn, create a new, desired behavior.

How do anchors get created? It's simple. Anytime you

have an intense feeling that causes you to go into a certain state of mind, whatever is happening while you are in that state of mind gets imprinted on your psyche. For example, as a teen, you and your best friend go to a concert together. Still, years later, every time you hear a song from that band, you think of your best friend.

A negative anchor can be triggered by something without your being aware that it is there—at least not consciously. For example, a song playing in the background may trigger and old feeling of sadness and depression. That is what anchoring is all about.

Advertising creates anchors all the time. Why do people smoke? The tobacco companies used TV—before cigarette ads were banned—to link smoking with feeling good. They used celebrities in their TV ads. They showed the smokers as being more loved, elegant, and sexy when they were smoking. Marlon Brando and James Dean made smoking look *cool* on the big screen—and the Marlboro man on TV and in print ads made smoking more manly and rugged. This visually suggested that smoking was an accepted social habit and doing it always made you look cool and feel good—and made you more popular.

There are many kinds of positive and negative anchors. Let's discuss how they work.

Step One: If you want to create an anchor for someone, the first thing you want to do is put the person in the state of mind that you want to anchor. For example, if you want to anchor someone with a feeling of pride, ask them to recall a time in their life when they felt really proud, then have them "step back into" that experience—as if they were there. Literally and physically put them in that state of mind by asking them to recreate it—the words they would be saying, the type of breathing they would exhibit.

Step Two: Once the person is fully connected to the feeling you want to anchor, the next thing you must do is provide a unique stimulus. You could touch a person gently on the shoulder and make a distinct noise while they are feeling "proud." Ask them to show you their posture when they are feeling proud. While they stand that way, touch their shoulder, make that unique noise, and then ask them to speak the way they speak when they feel proud. When they experience the peak of speaking in that uplifted, proud tone of voice, touch their shoulder, and again, make the distinct noise. Do this over and over again, while they are at the peak of this experience.

Step Three: You now have an anchor, so you want to get the person into a neutral state to see if it works. Do this by asking that person to just change the position of their body and move around.

Step Four: Test the anchor. Touch that spot on the person and make the unique noise. Notice what happens with their body. Does their proud gaze return? Do they smile? Does their body snap back into a similar position? If your anchor works, any time you "launch" it on the person, they will immediately go into the state of mind that you established with the anchor.

Make sure that when you establish the anchor, you do it when they are in that peak intense state of mind. If you anchor when they are not conducive, then the effect will be diminished. To have a potent anchor, you must trigger when they are at the strongest, most intense emotional state of mind.

When you initiate the anchor, there are variables that are significant determinants of how effective the anchor will be: the tone and volume of your voice, the look on your face, the softness or strength of your touch, and whether the person is at the peak of their experience.

Let's consider the metaphor of the feelings we associate with a roller-coaster ride. You don't want to anchor someone as they are on the way down that first hill; you don't want to do it as they are heading up the incline; you want to anchor them right at the top—at the apex of the incline. Getting this timing right is somewhat of an art.

You will want to practice your technique, so that you become as effective as possible. Try looking someone in the eyes as you practice this, and notice the look and excitement in their eyes to gauge their peak time. You will learn to note that peak time, and you will get better with each attempt.

You also want to have a unique stimulus. The more unique the stimulus, the more effective the anchor. And you don't always have to go through the process of "putting" people in that state of mind. Sometimes you can just "catch" them there. For example, if you "catch" someone laughing hysterically, go up and anchor them. While they are laughing, touch their elbow and make a unique sound. The reason that you don't *just* touch their elbow or *just* make the unique noise is that by having *both* the sound and the touch, the stimulus will be more effective. You could come back a few minutes later when the person has stopped laughing, make the unique sound, touch their elbow, and they will start to smile and laugh again. It is literally programmed into their nervous system.

You also *could* have shaken their hand while they were laughing, then come back and done it again, and it would trigger laughter again. The weakness with this anchor though, is that a lot of people are going to shake their hands, and they are going to be in many different states of mind as that happens. As a result, shaking their hand is not a unique enough stimulus.

Make sure you use the touch of an elbow, or a certain tone of voice, or a look that the person has never seen. That way it will have long-lasting power.

In order to have an anchor be effective, you need to replicate it effectively. If you anchor someone with a touch of their elbow and make a unique sound, you have to do it again and use the exact same touch and tone of voice.

Anchoring may sound difficult at first, but you will soon realize that it's hard *not* to anchor. You are anchoring constantly, but now you will be more conscious of it. Conscious, effective anchoring is one of the most important tools you can use to enhance everything you do in your life.

I have a couple more scenarios of anchoring to share. I used the anchor to change *someone else's* mindset. I have a close friend who purchased a house at the peak of the real estate boom. After the boom, his house began decreasing in value, and eventually was worth less than what he had paid for it. A couple of years later, things became even more dire. The value continued to decrease, and in addition, his income dropped significantly due to a job change. Home values were not going to rebound, and he felt that it just didn't make sense for him to keep a house that was so difficult for him to afford. He was considering not making the payments any longer and letting the bank take the house into foreclosure—but he hated the idea of doing this for a couple of reasons. He had already lost a house to foreclosure several years earlier due to a job loss. He didn't want to relive that depressing that feeling of losing another house. He also had done a number of improvements to the house. It fit him very nicely, and the place really felt like "home."

He talked to me about his dilemma. I encouraged him to make the decision of letting the bank take the house, based on the financial facts. I said, "I know you love this house, and it's going to be somewhat depressing to make that decision and actually move. Here are some things to consider that might help ease the pain. The house has a fairly steep driveway, and a very steep yard to mow." In this case, the *driveway* and the *steep yard* are both anchors.

Up until now he had enjoyed those features of the house for certain reasons. They were not negatives to him, because he had represented them as positives to himself. I said, "Here is what I want you to think from this day forward. Every time you come home and you drive up that driveway, I want you to say out loud—with passion—this statement. "*I hate this driveway, and what it's doing to my transmission. I can't wait to get out of this house.*" And, every week when you mow the lawn (in the area of the country he lived in, you have to mow your lawn every week of the year), say to yourself out loud—with passion, "*I hate mowing this lawn. It has such a steep slope and is so difficult to mow, I hate it, and I never want to mow this lawn again.*"

Within a month, he was so ready to move that he started staying at his girlfriend's house more than his own. He had dramatically changed his mindset about what that house meant to him. He turned his despair (over losing the house) into excitement, and he couldn't wait to get out. This shows how, if you learn to change the way you represent things to yourself, you can change the quality of your life at will.

In this second scenario, I used the anchor to change *my* mindset. For as long as I can remember, I have struggled with always being "in a hurry," and never feeling I accomplished as much in a day as I wanted. I was always feeling rushed, because I was forever trying to fit in "one more thing" before I left for a meeting—or wherever I needed to be. When I was on the road, I would inevitably find myself behind a slow driver, and I would be anxious to get around them. In essence, I used those cars as anchors to make myself frustrated.

One day I decided, *This is not a good habit pattern for me. I am using these anchors for negative, rather than positive.* I decided to change the way I used this anchor (the car). I started changing my representation of what it meant to see a car on the road in front of me, blocking my progress. I started using a visualization technique. I visualized the car getting smaller and smaller, and getting farther and farther away. I used my car's brakes as one of my anchors. Every time I saw myself getting close to a car, I programmed myself to tap the brake, and visualize the car getting smaller and farther away. Then I would play one of my favorite songs in my head—one that always put a smile on my face. What a difference! Now, instead of getting frustrated and anxious when I see the heavy traffic, I touch the brake, hear a great song, and I smile.

You now possess the tools to alter your feelings and

behaviors in any situation by changing what you represent to yourself. This chapter has given you the additional tools to use your mind and body to reprogram your behaviors long-term. Anchoring is one of the most powerful tools you can employ. Now you know how to change your state of mind and your behaviors, and you can anchor yourself to results that are consistent with the state of mind you wish to have.

Anchor yourself to happiness and contentment.

Think it through, and do it today.

Health, Fitness and Energy

Being physically fit is a vital aspect of a good, healthy self-image. It is a tremendous way to build your self-esteem. The better shape you're in, the better you feel about yourself.

Energy is the source of our actions. Nothing happens without it. The more energy that pulsates within, the more personal power you'll obtain. Energy is the fuel that lifts your "plane" off the ground and carries you to success.

Just as physical energy is critical, if you run out of *emotional fuel* while you are climbing the "hill" of success, you will quickly coast back downhill. This happens to a lot of people. Do you remember a day when you awoke feeling tired and had a hard time waking up and getting started? I know for me, if I wake up like that, I am definitely not sitting on the edge of the bed slapping my hands and thinking, *What a wonderful day to change the world!* For most people, when they feel like this, their first thought is, *I wonder if I can call in sick today?*

Everything that you do to improve your physical well-being will have a positive impact on your self-confidence. In fact, every effort you make to take care of yourself will raise your self-esteem. Whenever you take specific, concrete action toward self-improvement, your self-esteem increases. You consider yourself more valuable and worthwhile.

On the other hand, if you let yourself get run-down, you will have a nagging feeling that you're not taking responsibility for yourself. Whenever you place your career or anything else ahead of your health, you undoubtedly shorten your life-span. So what value have you created for yourself, if you won't be around long enough to fully enjoy the success?

Nature demands balance in life. Whenever this balance falters, your mind and body will suffer the consequences. With high levels of health and energy, you feel terrific about yourself and are more competent and capable of meeting challenges. With high levels of health and energy, you are more positive and self- assured. You are sharper and more alert, your sleep is deeper, richer quality rest.

When you are trim and physically fit, you are more relaxed and more effective in your interactions with others. You are more admired and respected. Most of all, you respect yourself. You know you made the sacrifice and had the self-discipline to transform and maintain yourself.

As stated, ***you become what you think about most.*** The more thoughts you have about taking care of your body, the more mentally healthy you will be, but remember, ***you also become***

what you eat.

Your body is a chemical factory, and it is always creating new cells and eliminating old cells and waste. Your body is controlled by your nervous system, which regulates the chemical balance in billions of cells every minute of every day. It is nothing short of miraculous. But your body, like any factory, can only manufacture high quality finished products when supplied with high quality raw materials.

The measure of your physical health is your level of energy. Everything that you do requires energy, and the more energy you have, the more you'll try new things—and the more you'll accomplish.

Energy is produced in your body with the help of four vital ingredients. The first is food. The second is water. Third is aerobic exercise. And fourth is a good, healthy mindset.

The starting point of feeling fantastic is to eat the right, healthy foods and drink the proper amounts of water. Fortunately, there is no shortage of information on what constitutes a proper diet. There have been some exciting scientific breakthroughs over the last several years regarding diet and nutrition. Robert Haas, author of *Eat to Win*, wrote about a high performance diet and the fact that it consists of approximately seventy-five percent complex carbohydrates, fifteen percent proteins, and ten percent fats.

There is now an avalanche of research and proof that you can eat more than you might think and still lose weight, as long as you eat foods that the body burns off, rather than stores. The ideal diet for high performance consists of lots of fruits, vegetables, whole grains, and nuts. The more colorful the fruits and vegetables, the more minerals and vitamins they contain, and the better they are for you. Fruits and vegetables are roughage that helps keep your system clean and light by continually eliminating toxins and waste products.

Whole grains and nuts have the same impact and also contain proteins and fats in limited quantities. Simply shifting your diet away from bacon and eggs to fruit and whole grains will help you to be sharper for the entire first half of your day.

Harvey and Marilyn Diamond wrote a book several years ago called, *Fit for Life*. The book was on the New York Times Best Sellers List. It sold millions of copies based on its unorthodox—at the time—suggestions on diets. When it was released, many nutritionists disagreed with the book's teachings, and it was considered quite controversial. The Diamonds contended that the greatest consumer of energy in the body is the process of digestion. If you can make digesting easier, by combining your foods in such a way that they don't require as much energy to break down, you will have more energy available for other things. If you eat fruits, vegetables, whole grains and nuts, because they are natural, they will digest faster, and you will feel lighter and more energetic.

The Diamonds claimed that when you digest proteins, your body creates acids to break them down; and with starches, your body creates alkaline to break them down. But when you eat starches and proteins together; such as meat and potatoes, eggs and toast, or fish and rice; your body creates both acids and alkaline, each of which neutralizes the other in the stomach, which results in your food failing to digest. The digestive process is brought to a halt.

Your stomach is determined to break the food down before it passes it into the small intestines. When the acids and the alkaline neutralize each other, the body works vigorously to produce even more acids and more alkaline. This draws blood and energy from other parts of the body, making you feel tired and drowsy after a big meal. But if you eat proteins with vegetables, or starches with vegetables, rather than proteins and starches together, this digestive problem doesn't occur. You can eat larger quantities and still feel light and clear-headed. We simply eat too much protein and fat. The body doesn't need as much as we take in to build new cells, and both proteins and fats are extremely hard to digest. They contain more calories per ounce than any other food. If we take in more than we require, the body uses an enormous amount of energy to break it down, and then stores the extra protein and fat for later use. This is a very different habit pattern than most of us learned as we grew up. There are still a number of people that will disagree with this dietary philosophy, but if you consciously keep this in mind, it will be easier to begin the habit of eating healthier.

In Dr. Robert Jorgensen's book titled, *Eat and Grow Thin*, he states that the greatest enemies to our health are fat and cholesterol. And we can dramatically increase our energy levels and reduce our weight—at the same time—by reducing fats of all kinds.

The body does need a small amount of cholesterol, but the average person consumes far too much fat in their daily diet. Jorgensen talks about the amounts of butter, margarine, and oils we use in preparing many of our foods. It has become a "not so good" habit in an effort to enhance the flavor of our food. The bottom line is that if we are going to be healthy, we must train our taste buds so that we can enjoy foods that are healthy for us.

A great and easy healthy habit is the drinking of six to eight glasses of water every day. I know that we have all heard that statement for so long that we have learned to let it go "in one ear and out the other," as my mother used to say, but it is a very worthwhile habit.

Many people start the day with coffee, then move to soft drinks throughout the afternoon, and polish the day off with a few cocktails or beers. Not all—but most—of these drinks contain large amounts of sugar. We need to start the day by drinking one or two glasses of water, and then have a few more large glasses throughout the day. If you think about it, six to eight glasses is only three to four bottles of water a day. Not really that much—to become really healthy.

If you truly want to be healthy and in a state of **peak performance**, you need to limit coffee and soft drinks and satisfy your thirst with water. The evidence is overwhelming that drinking large quantities of water has a dramatic positive effect on your health. When I attended Tony Robbins,' *Unleash the Power Within*, four-day seminar event, he said confidently, "*Try eating mainly fruits, vegetables, and nuts—and drinking primarily water—for thirty days...you will notice the difference*."

When you eat the right foods in the right combinations, there are three ingredients you need to avoid. They have been referred to as the **three white poisons:** sugar, salt, and white flour.

The average American consumes almost two hundred

pounds of sugar every year in the form of desserts, soft drinks, alcoholic beverages, etc. They are simple carbohydrates that give you a *temporary* lift, but a long-term drop in energy. The consumption of sugar causes your pancreas to secrete large amounts of insulin into your blood stream, so that it can soak up the additional sugar. In "overreacting" to protect you from this imbalance, the pancreas secretes too much insulin. The result is that it extracts even more blood sugar, and you are left feeling weaker than you were before you ate the candy bar or drank the soft drink. By ceasing the consumption of extra sugars, eliminating the desserts, (and getting the sweetness that you crave from fruits and juices) you will feel better from the first day.

The second white poison is salt. Salt is used to enhance the flavor of food and also to preserve shelf-life at the supermarket. The average person needs about two pounds of salt per year; however, the average American consumes more than twenty-five pounds of salt per year! Salt is the most common product used to preserve what are essentially "dead" foods on the supermarket shelves. Many products have salt as a primary ingredient, and you get enough salt in your diet naturally without adding much more than a pinch when you are cooking. Many people get into the habit, early in life, of putting salt on everything—even before they taste it. However, when you stop adding salt, you begin to taste a wider array of flavors than you have in the past.

We all know that consuming too much salt is harmful and it leads to hypertension, irritability, high blood pressure, and fatigue. It is also a major cause of water retention. Many people are several pounds overweight because excess salt causes the body to retain water. If you stop consuming extra salt and simultaneously start drinking eight glasses of water each day, you will quickly drop a few pounds and start to wash out all the extra salt your body has stored. In any case, the more water you drink and the less salt you consume, the better you will feel, the sounder you will sleep, and the more energy you will have.

The third white poison is white flour. The problem is that white flour is basically an inert substance. It has been made white by bleaching it to the point that it has been thoroughly "cleansed" of all nutrients. Years ago, when consumers complained that white bread contained no food value, the bakers responded by adding vitamins to the products, labeling them "enriched." Vitamins are poured into the ingredients, but promptly killed in the baking process. What you end up with has no food value at all, aside from a few carbohydrates.

If you shift from white breads to whole grain breads, you will get more vitamins, more flavors, more energy, and better digestion. I eat bread that is made from a variety of sprouts and seeds, and mostly organic ingredients. The flavor is awesome, and the nutrition values are excellent.

Years ago, the New York Times had a great article on eating less and living longer. They called it "Under-eating without Undernourishment." The story was about a study that was conducted with lab rats that were put on lean diets. These rats lived up to fifty percent longer than the rats that were allowed to eat whatever they wanted.

The researchers also found that people who ate lean, light foods—and ate less of them—were much healthier, had more energy, needed less sleep, and had better sex drives. More than anything else, eating lean products that contained high levels of nutrients, reduced the incidence of diseases of all kinds. And if the research is any indication, eating lean may be the key to increasing the average human life span from seventy-five years up to a hundred years or more.

We need to adopt the principle of **eating to live**, rather than **living to eat**. An article on Yahoo's news page in June, 2011 said that most Americans are eating at least a third more food today than they did in 1975. And that the food we are eating today is much more processed than it was in 1975 and has less nutrition. If we are eating a third more food today, it is no wonder the obesity rate continues to climb. I have gotten into the habit of using a food-based liquid vitamin supplement. This is a good addition to my meals that really helps me feel better.

When anthropologists examine the lifestyles of men and women from around the world where it is common to live beyond the age of one hundred, they find that these people have three things in common.

One is that they eat lots of fruits, nuts, vegetables, and whole grain products; and the meat they eat is lean and in small amounts, rather than it being the main portion.

Secondly, they all live in areas of the world where the normal day's activities include a lot of walking and physical activity.

The third factor they have in common is their culture. In these societies, older people are highly respected and are strongly connected to community life. They feel valuable and worthwhile, which instills a positive self-image.

One final point to make with regard to nutrition is the importance of regular elimination. A diet filled with fruits, vegetables, nuts, and whole grains not only gives you the nutrition you need, but it also ensures that you get the fiber your digestive system needs to function properly.

I am fortunate to live in an area of the United States that allows more diversity in medical practitioners than other parts of the country. We have medical practices that are run by; Nurse Practitioners, Naturopathic Physicians, and Physiatrists. We also have access to a wide scope of treatments, including botanical, nutritional, acupuncture, and many more that I am just learning about. They bring different theories to the practice of health and well-being.

I take my health very seriously and I believe maintaining my body is much more important than most people believe. I go to a Chiropractor on a regular basis. I also go to a Naturopathic Clinic regularly where I get a Vitamin IV bag and receive other treatments that I had not heard of prior to moving to Arizona. The clinic staff stresses the importance of regular elimination as part of being healthy. One of the ways they suggest cleaning out your system is to do a sea-salt purge. Two teaspoons of sea-salt in a quart of warm water drank first thing in the morning will go through and flush out your entire system in approximately one hour. I personally use a product called *Colon Clenz* that I get at Walmart.

I have a good friend here in the Phoenix area, Patrick Schinzel, who holds a PhD in Pharmacology. Patrick is a Pharmacist who is so fascinated by the human body that he spent a number of years studying the effects of the food we eat, the water we drink, and the addition of minerals to our diet—minerals that we don't get from our food. He spent time studying under Dr. Robert O.Young, a top research scientist in the field of cellular nutrition, about the make-up of our bodies and how they function. I drink a "green drink" every day that I learned about from Tony Robbins. I heard that Dr. Young was the one who introduced Tony Robbins to the "green drink." Patrick and I were talking about the "green drink" one day, and he suggested that I add a specific salt mixture and some clay to my green drink for my body to get the maximum benefit, and for optimum nutrition and cleansing. It has been a great addition to my regular diet and has made a significant difference in the way I feel. When Patrick and I get together, we can talk for hours nonstop about food, health, and having an awesome attitude toward life. Most people eavesdropping probably think we are "crazy."

I have talked to many people over the years who have tried cleansing diets and fasts. They were always astonished to find that even after a week, their bodies were still eliminating toxins and waste products that had been stored up over the years. Cleansing diets and fasts are certainly beneficial on an occasional basis, but switching to a regular diet of fruits, nuts, vegetables, whole grains and water will keep your internal system clean and your bodily functions regular. As a result, you will feel more positive, clear-headed, energetic, and effective. It has made a dramatic difference in my life, and I highly recommend it.

A critical element of health and fitness as it relates to your self-image is your weight. There is nothing that diminishes your self-esteem faster than being overweight in a world that respects and admires fitness and thinness. No one is perfect, and we need to get the thought of "perfection" out of our heads. At the same time, being *reasonably* healthy and *reasonably* fit does require that we maintain a *reasonable* weight.

Oprah Winfrey has had a positive impact on the world in many ways. One of the most profound effects came from her "introducing" me—and the world—to Dr. Mehmet Oz. I believe that Dr. Oz's knowledge and mindset toward health,(shared through his primte-time show) will forever change the way the world views health and well-being. I watch very little TV because little of it truly feeds my mind with good, positive information. The *Dr. Oz Show* should be a "must watch" for anyone who wants to be truly healthy. I have read a number of his books, and I highly recommend them as part of your ongoing education for life.

I had the opportunity to watch one of the *Dr. Oz Show* episodes where he discussed how to lessen the risk of heart disease and cancer. I was amazed when Dr. Oz said that he believed the cause of eighty-five percent of heart disease and cancer was lifestyle related. He said if we changed our habits, we could dramatically change our risk of heart disease and cancer.

The list of habits he suggested people change were: to stop smoking, drink limited amounts of alcohol, reduce the amounts of fatty foods in our diet, and get regular strenuous exercise. Wow! In a world where these habits are major killers, I thought, *What a worthwhile change in our lifestyle that could save so many lives*. I have seen so much good conversation about having a healthy mind and body on the *Dr. Oz Show.* I'm happy it has such a high viewership.

On one show Dr. Oz discussed obesity. He said that

for every pound we are overweight, our heart has to pump our blood one more mile, and that every pound we are overweight shortens our life.

I want to make sure I say loud and clear, *no one is perfect and we all have areas of our life that we can improve upon.* However, if we truly want to be happy, being physically fit is part of that depth of happiness. You *can* take control of your weight, *if* you commit to being healthy. For most of us, the way we become overweight is from eating more food—calories—than we burn. There are some exceptions to this, but for most people this is true.

If you want to lose weight, you must increase your burn rate and decrease your caloric intake. You start getting down to your correct weight by setting it as a goal and mapping out a clear and well-thought out lifestyle change to achieve it. The real key though is to reduce your intake on one hand and burn off more calories on the other through regular exercise. This protocol lowers your automatic set-point, the weight at which your body stabilizes. This is when your body automatically adjusts to a *point* where you can stop watching what you eat. You can only lower your set-point through exercise.

Exhaustive research has shown that diets don't work. The reason the diets don't work, is that people typically go through what is called a "starve and binge" cycle. They deny themselves food until they are "starving," and then they reward themselves by "binging" on the food they denied themselves. If you look at food as a reward for any behavior, your chances of maintaining weight loss is almost zero. The key to permanent weight loss is to change your entire attitude about eating. Change the types of foods you eat and the quantities. Make the firm decision that you will be so involved in achieving goals that are important to you, eating will become a secondary consideration. You will gradually lower your set-point, and ultimately you will be eating so well, that you won't have to worry about your weight again.

Of course, you can't have optimum health, fitness, and energy, without regular, proper exercise. Proper, consistent exercise is absolutely imperative to being and feeling healthy. Regular exercise causes your brain to produce the body's "natural morphine" called endorphins. It gives you a natural "high" and feeling of wellness. I can't say that I just love to exercise; but I know that if I don't exercise, I don't feel as good as I want to, I don't look as good as I want to, and I don't sleep as well as I need to. So, for me, it is a lifestyle that takes discipline to maintain. Even for people who don't like exercise and haven't done much, you can eventually become positively addicted to exercise, because you will feel so good physically and emotionally.

The **law of life** simply says, **if you don't use it, you lose it**. The more you use it, the better it performs for you, and the longer it lasts. To feel at your best, you need three key components: strength, flexibility, and endurance.

The wonderful thing about exercise is that although you may feel worn out for a few days while you adjust to your new schedule, after those first few days, you will begin to feel more energetic and alert. The cure for low levels of energy is high levels of exercise. The more you work out, the more energy you have.

The more you exercise, the more sins it covers up in regards to our eating habits. Aerobic instructors say that you should work out at least three times per week for more than 20 minutes each time. You only begin to get what is called the "aerobic effect" after twenty minutes of exercise. In the first twenty minutes, you burn off glucose in your blood stream. Every minute after those first twenty, you will burn extra fat that has been stored from overeating in the past, and you will be working toward lowering your set-point.

After you have finished exercising aerobically, your body continues to burn calories at a higher rate for another five hours. When you combine exercise with the correct diet, the combination can be amazing. In less than a month, you will be a different person. Your posture will improve, your smile will be bigger, your eyes will shine brighter, and you will feel terrific about yourself.

The two most common times to exercise are in the morning, before you start your day, and in the evening. Although these may be the most practical times, it isn't critical when you do it, just as long as you do it as a regular part of your life. Write it into your calendar as a regular appointment. And by the way, talking to your friends at the gym for an hour is not considered aerobic exercise.

Two significant keys to health and fitness are proper rest and a proper attitude. To get proper rest, you need to sleep eight hours a night. I used to burn the candle at both ends. For years, I rarely got eight hours of sleep, and eventually my health started suffering. There were a few times when I got ill enough that I ended up in the hospital, or I was literally so burned out that I was forced to rest for a period of time before I could resume work. Believe me, a lack of sleep is severely damaging to my health, so I almost always get eight to nine hours of sleep now.

From time to time I have something going on that keeps me from getting a good night's sleep, and I really can tell the difference. I usually make up for it the next night with an extra hour or two of sleep. You need to take regular breaks and vacations, but sometimes one of the best thing you can do is go to bed early and get a good night's sleep.

When you feel you don't have time to rest, that is when it is most important for you to get away and relax. Many people take a full day off each week to rest and relax. You will perform far better and get more done on the other six days if you take that time off, than you ever would if you worked straight through.

One of the most important lifestyle changes that I have implemented for myself is to take time to have fun—to take the time for myself *without* the interference of work. It took me more time than I would like to admit to allow myself to do this and to realize the value in it.

The final key is having a great mental attitude. A cheerful and sunny disposition leads to a healthy and vibrant body. As I have said several times before, just the act of smiling makes you feel good. The way you see yourself and the way you use your body are indispensable to your mental and physical health. So keep yourself optimistic, keep your body moving, and develop a level of energy that is unstoppable.

Goals Create a Compelling Future

The power of knowing what you want and being committed to it.

As I have watched and studied about some of the most successful people in the world, I noticed a common thread; they all had a very clear vision for their life. They had specific goals and compelling reasons why they wanted to achieve those goals.

Let's take me for example. I grew up in a very poor family, and the living conditions in my neighborhood were some of the worst in the country. As I mentioned earlier, I had made some very clear statements to myself, as well as to my family and friends. I was disgusted with living in run-down houses. I was tired being broke and eating crappy food. I was burnt out on having one pair of shoes, one pair of blue jeans, and one or two shirts—that were all worn out and didn't fit well because they were too big or too small.

I shouted from the rooftops, "*I will work as hard as I have to work, but I will not live like this when I grow up. I will be rich when I grow up."* At that age, I didn't have a clearly defined plan, but I sure had lots of compelling reasons for getting out of the life that we had at the time.

We can all learn to put clearly defined plans together, and as time goes on, we will get better at defining our goals and writing out the steps necessary to achieve those goals. We need to *start* with those compelling reasons—that driving force—to make the changes we *must* in an effort to live the life we dream about. Those dreams—those compelling futures—are the key to getting us to take massive action. Again, as I have talked about before, **become a dreamer**. Dare to think the thoughts of unlimited potential for yourself. Fantasize about the unimaginable and write it all down, as if you plan to achieve it. This is the beginning of creating your own compelling future.

A great exercise that is to develop a list of goals that you can get excited enough about to get you to take that *massive* action. Make a list of a dozen things that get your blood pumping. The list doesn't need to be realistic, just make a list. Then write out each of the twelve things on its own separate piece of paper. I think it's necessary that you list twelve things—*subjects*—because as you do this exercise you will find that some are more compelling than others. Once you contemplate them for a while, you may revise your list, some things may fall off the list. You can't do everything at once, but to live a fulfilling, long life you need to have some variety to keep your interest and excitement level up. Also what interests you today will change as you go through life. You may find that one of the things that was not a priority earlier in life, may become a priority later. Do this exercise often to make sure you are on track and to clarify what's important to you. By the way, these exercises will take some time and you probably won't get more than one done at a time, but if you really want to change your life—well, no one said it was going to be easy.

After you have written the subject (what interests you) at the top of the page, go into a dark room, close your eyes, and start thinking about that subject. Fantasize…as if you have no limits to what you can achieve. Imagine how you could make money doing whatever it is, and how much fun you would have doing it, until you just can't write any more.

After you have done this for all twelve subjects, review your interests and prioritize them based on what engages you most. Talk about this list with a friend, relative, or counselor and discuss them at length to get someone else's perspective on your thoughts. If you do discuss the subjects with another, make sure he or she is someone who will look on this exercise you are doing in a positive light, so that you don't get discouraged.

My mother told me, "You can do anything you want as long as you are willing to work hard enough to make it happen. And never let anyone tell you that you can't do something that you are really excited about."

So now that you have this list of twelve subjects, you need to narrow the list down to one or two things—with a plan for how you are going to *get there*.

Let's look at an example of someone who has gone from having very little to becoming a superstar: Madonna. Let me preface what I am about to say with a "disclaimer" of sorts: I have never spoken to Madonna, however, I do know enough about the music business and promotion to have a pretty good idea of at least some of what she went through in order to for her to rise to the pinnacle of the music industry.

Madonna was born and raised in Michigan. Her parents were not rich. She had a dream of becoming an entertainer. The town where she lived was not exactly on the "list of cities" that turned out highly successful entertainers, so in 1977 she moved to New York City to pursue a career in dance.

I am sure she went to New York with little money, and likely got a job waiting tables or something similar, while she tried to connect with the people who could help her get started in her career. She may have gone to some venues where they played live music, made some friends, and asked them who they knew in the music business. She likely wasn't the singer or dancer that she is today, so she certainly wasn't ready for the Blonde Ambition Tour—yet. She probably did a few auditions that she got turned down for. That rejection might have turned some people into quitters, but not Madonna. My guess is that she got even more determined, so she practiced more and more, and got better and better. Just like Colonel Sanders and his chicken recipe, Madonna had to go to audition after audition until she got her first job in the industry. I am sure she continued going to as many music venues as she could, meeting a variety of people, until she started making some things happen for herself. The more people she met, the more connections she made, and the more she made happen, the closer she got to her goal; all the while, practicing her singing and songwriting. She got an acting part in a movie that was not a blockbuster, but it "got her noticed" and got her introduced to even more people. The rest of the story is more of the same continued hard work, until she became one of the most well-known superstars in the world.

I guarantee you that Madonna worked her butt off more; put in more hours working her "side" jobs to support herself; practiced more; went to more auditions—basically put more hours and effort into her dream each week than most people devote in a month to achieve their dreams.

So, was Madonna *born* a superstar and just needed to get noticed, or was she someone who had a huge dream and worked tirelessly to hone her skills so she could reach her goal?

We all know the answer to that question! She didn't innately *know* all the venues where she would find these people she needed. She didn't just *know* how to network and find the right people to get where she needed to be. She learned that skill as she went—by asking. No one *knows* everything, and no one has all the answers; but if you learn to ask questions, and you learn to recognize the *right* people to ask, you will eventually learn what you need to know, and get where you want to go.

I guarantee that you *will* get some wrong answers along the way, and you *will* make some mistakes; but if you have a compelling enough dream and enough faith in yourself, nothing will keep you down for long.

On one of his tapes, Zig Ziglar talked about a reporter who was doing a story on H. L. Hunt, one of the richest people in the world at the time. The reporter asked Mr. Hunt, "Here we are in one of the richest countries in the world, and yet we know that ninety-five percent of us will die broke. Why do you believe that to be true?"

Mr. Hunt said, "The reason is that most people never decide what it is that they want, and so if they never set a goal, they certainly will never reach for success."

Here we are in a time when opportunity is available to so many all over the world, yet so many don't accept the responsibility to take control of their lives, set goals, and create visions for themselves that excite them enough to take action.

J.C. Penney said, "Give me a stock clerk with a goal, and I'll give you a man who'll make history. But give me a man without a goal, and I'll give you a stock clerk."

You must learn to set goals. You must learn to devise detailed road maps of how to attain your goals.

I make a list everyday of what I plan to achieve that day. I also make a list of things I plan to achieve that month, as well as goals for that year, and the next five years.

We are goal-seeking individuals. Goals give us purpose and direction. When we aren't making progress in the direction of our goals, we begin to stall and slide back. There is an old adage: "*You are either growing or dying, there is no in-between.*" Without goals, the quality of a person's life begins to deteriorate. They feel there is nothing to work for, and they become sullen and depressed. **The only way to have long- term happiness and success is to have long-term goals.**

There was a study done in 1953 at Yale University, where researchers interviewed the graduating members of the class and asked them about their goals. Only three percent of them had a goal list or a plan. Twenty years later, in 1973, a follow-up interview was done. The researchers discovered some interesting facts. Those who had set goals, the three percent, seemed to be better adjusted emotionally, socially, and with their families. They also found a measurable difference financially. The three percent who had set goals had more financial wealth than the rest of the class combined.

How do we explain this discrepancy just from someone setting some goals? The answer is, that when you make it clear in your conscious mind what it is that you want(goal-setting) your subconscious mind takes over and causes everything that you see, hear, and do to be in line with your preordained outcome. If you visualize your goals in detail as you set them, you literally program them into your nervous system. I can't stress it enough—**please write out your goals and how you plan to achieve them.**

There are always going to be things that you desire, but the world won't end if you don't get them. So you must clarify the difference between those things you *can live without* and your *must-have* list. As you do this, you answer the question, *What must I achieve? You* will start to clarify what it is that you really want. Keep in mind, if you have more than ten *must-have*'s, you may feel overwhelmed and won't be able to get yourself to take action.

And remember, it's okay to want a luxury car and an opulent house, but make sure that you include the rest of what you *really* want, so you end up getting the most out of life. I do this practice every year to keep myself on track and to adapt to life changes. If you do this annually, you will see at the end of each year that you have acquired and accomplished a number of things on that year's list.

Zig Ziglar says, "Go as far as you can see and then when you get there, you will always be able to see farther." Frequently we see movie stars or wealthy people who have everything they dreamed of, yet they commit suicide because they are unhappy. They are unhappy because they didn't take the time to build the foundation of self-esteem and happiness, before—or during— their quest for fame and fortune.

As you are using the dark room technique, ask yourself these questions: *What is my purpose or my mission? What is it that I really want?* Visualize your life exactly the way you'd like it to be in specific areas of your life.

Home: What would your home look like? Where would you live? What would the furniture be like? Who would live there with you? What kind of view would you have? What color would your home be painted? And at this stage, don't worry how you are going to be able to accomplish all this. Just be honest with yourself—ask what it is that you really want.

Career: What would you like to be? Where would you be working? What would your financial situation be? How much money would you have? How much in savings? How much income?

Family and friends: What would your relation-ships be like? How many people in your family?

Your body and your physical health: What would you look like? What shape would you be in physically?

Community and community service: If you were living in the ideal community, what would be going on?

Goals are measurable: *I am going to own a 2500 square foot vacation home in Hawaii in the Kahala neighborhood by*

December 31, 2015. Goals are specific: *I am going to be singing on stage at Tootsie's in Nashville on the night of July 15th, 2012.*

I was at a Jack Canfield seminar when he told a story of a friend, Monty Roberts, who raised thoroughbred horses on a huge ranch in California. He said that Monty probably sold six million dollars worth of horses a year. Monty's father had been an itinerant horse trainer. When Monty was in school, he and his father lived in a trailer, because they didn't have a house. They spent all of their time going from track to track. One day, Monty's teacher asked his students to write a paper on what dreams they wanted to fulfill when they grew up. Monty wrote that he wanted to own a ranch and sell horses. He also drew a detailed picture of the house and the horses he dreamed of owning, and he handed in his paper. The teacher gave Monty and "F" on his paper and told him to see him after class.

The teacher told Monty he had to realize that he was the son of an itinerant horse trainer, and there was no way he could become a rancher. He told Monty it was impossible, and that if he re-wrote the paper "realistically," he would give him a new grade.

Monty took the paper home, asked his Dad what he should do, and his dad said, "You need to write what's in your heart." Monty struggled with this for over a week, but ultimately handed in his original paper and said, "I'll take the F, because this is my dream."

Canfield has been to Monty's ranch. He said that it was "Two hundred of the finest acres you'll ever see…it's huge and the house is the exact floor plan Monty drew when he was in high school." Jack said that when Monty first told him the story, he also told him that about two summers ago, the teacher who gave him that F brought thirty kids to camp out at the ranch. Monty said that the teacher finally did apologize and said, "Thank God you had enough courage not to listen to me."

There is an old adage, *"If you don't have any plans, you are going to work for someone who does."*

Brian Tracy says that if you *verbalize* your goals, you are more likely to achieve them than you would be if you kept them to yourself. But, if you *write down* your goals, then you are ten times more likely to achieve them. And, if you write down those same goals *every day*, then you are one hundred times more likely to achieve them. I also sign my name below each goal, to emphasize my commitment.

If you really want to achieve your goals, then I would make the extra effort to write them down every day. It's a great idea to write your goals down on small note cards, so you can have easy access to them throughout your day. Look at them several times a day.

Clear goals free you from the **law of accident**, the tendency for things to happen in a random and unpredictable ways. Goals will give you a clear sense of direction and knowledge that your life is self-determined. They channel your energy, and instill the sense that everything that happens is part of an organized plan—a plan that is taking you step-by-step toward the attainment of your goals.

Your ability to set goals and make plans for their accomplishment is really one of the most important skills of success. The regular habit of goal-setting and achieving those goals is probably more important than almost anything else you will ever learn.

Fear is the great enemy of self-confidence. Fear has always been the greatest enemy of mankind in many ways. Fear holds us back more than any other factor. It affects our subconscious and sabotages our intentions.

I have heard many people say, *I could never do that. I would never try that because I would be so afraid that I would fail and look stupid. I would feel so bad if I failed, I couldn't stand it*. Or, *I would be mortified if I asked that question and someone said they thought I had asked a dumb question.* No one wants to look or feel stupid or incompetent, but—**trying something and not achieving what you intended is just another way of practicing**.

As we get older, we are so afraid of criticism that it prevents us from trying. I have been in so many different industries and had to learn so many different things in life that I feel I have made more mistakes than most people make in an entire lifetime—and I still have half of my life left! I plan to try a few more industries before I quit, so I will undoubtedly make another lifetime of mistakes over the next several years.

But unlike some folks, I look at these mistakes as learning experiences—and I love to learn. If you find yourself having thoughts of inadequacy, you must learn to banish those thoughts and replace them with excitement about the new goals you have set for yourself.

Sometimes fears will manifest as rationalizations and excuses. You can find an excuse to not do just about anything.

You may say, "*I already know what my goals are, so I don't need to write them down.*" Or maybe some other negative self-talk such as, "*I am afraid that I won't reach my goal, so I am not going to write it down. I'll just feel worse if I write down my goals and then don't achieve them.*"

Sometimes fear will surface in the form of procrastination. You resolve to write out your goals or plans on the weekend, on your vacation, or sometime in the indefinite future. Then, like ninety-seven percent of Americans, you will never do it. You will rationalize and say, "*Well, considering my situation, writing down my goals wouldn't have made much of a difference anyway.*"

If the great enemy of self-confidence is fear, then the great enemy of human achievement is the **comfort zone**. Psychologists have found that we have a tendency to have this "zone" of behavior, or performance, where we are comfortable; where it is easy and safe to remain. We stop striving, we relax, and day-by-day, we develop the habits that lead to underachievement—and ultimately—failure.

The tragedy of the comfort zone is that it initially starts with us feeling comfortable, which in time, leads to feeling complacent. Complacency then leads to boredom—and to the question of, *Is this all there is?* Instead being an exciting adventure, life becomes a boring repetition. Staying in the comfort zone creates a state of frustration and unhappiness with their lives.

Deep down inside, the average person knows that there is something better than this. The Theory of Self-Determination states that *in every organism, there is an inborn drive toward the complete fulfillment of its inherent possibilities.* There is a nagging feeling inside that tells us there is far more that we can *have* and *do*.

Great men and women are those who **absolutely** believe they have a great purpose. They have a vision of something greater or better than their current circumstances. Personal greatness means having a sense of destiny or conviction that your thoughts are the only real limits to your possibilities.

In a five-year study of people considered to be leaders, it was discovered that each of the leaders consciously avoided the comfort zone by setting higher goals. They never allowed themselves to become complacent. They always strived to be more. This same mindset can be applied to each of us. To develop unshakable self-confidence, you need to *think of* and *see yourself as* a leader. Do what leaders do. Stretch yourself to the outermost boundaries of your potential. Work toward objectives that lead you to feel a sense of mastery and peak performance—and it all begins with a pad of paper, a pen, and your list of goals. The very act of writing your goals down sets the whole universe to work for you and activates all mental laws. The act of writing down challenging goals causes three things to happen.

1) Your self-confidence goes up immediately. The act of setting goals requires confidence—and also builds confidence. Having the courage to write down what you really want enhances your self-image and your self-esteem. The action itself generates a feeling of greater personal power and ability.

2) Goal setting actually gives you a burst of physical and mental energy. Your heart rate speeds up…it's exciting.

3) That you have committed the goals to paper dramatically increases the likelihood that you will achieve those goals. You cannot define a goal without simultaneously having the ability to attain it. Again, the most important question is, *How badly do you want it? What is your compelling reason?*

To perform at your best, your life must be in balance. You need to have goals in each area of your life. You need to move forward on things that are important to you and ensure that each of these things is in harmony with each other. The next step, once you have all your goals organized, is to prioritize them. Select the goals that are more important and put them at the top of your list. Finally and most importantly, select the one goal out of all of them that is most important. This goal is the one that, when accomplished, will lead to the attainment of all your other goals. It "breaks open the dam."

Single-minded concentration in the direction of your dream will intensify your desires and increase your momentum toward your goal. This "razor's edge" will activate the law of attraction and will begin to attract people and opportunities into your life that are in harmony with your goal. The more you think about it, the more it will dominate your life, and the more rapidly you will move toward it—and it towards you.

Your major goal must be measurable. It's a basic rule of life: *What gets measured gets done.* Make it clear, quantitative, and objective. When necessary, break it down into smaller parts so you can work on one part at a time. Your goals must have clear timelines. Select realistic, but challenging dates and write them down. If it is a long-term goal, set benchmarks every few months to review your progress.

Finally, create a structure of rewards when you reach milestones—and when you reach the final goal. You need to tie each goal to a reward, and each *part* of a goal to a smaller reward. The reward may be a new pair of shoes, a new suit, a new set of golf clubs, a vacation, or a new car. It may be something that profits your family, such as a family outing to a water amusement park.

Rewards make the process more fun and engaging. They act as an inner driver that propels you forward when the "going gets tough." Rewarding yourself is a very important part of staying motivated and excited. There is a unique feeling that comes from achieving something.

We have all heard the phrases, *the sweet smell of victory, savoring success,* and *take the time to smell the roses*. We are living such a fast-paced lifestyle, that we don't always slow down to celebrate our successes. Celebrating our life is one of the most valuable indications of having a healthy self-image. If you are excited about your life, then you have come to a great place.

When you go to work each week, you get *rewarded* with a paycheck. When your children do their household chores, you *reward* them with an allowance. Reading a book on self-improvement gives you a *rewarding* feeling, because you know you have done something to improve your life. We must remember to reward ourselves when we reach a milestone, so that we maintain the high level of excitement.

If you don't reward yourself, you are not positively

reinforcing your efforts. And if you are self-employed, and you don't have a boss to give you that reward, it is particularly important to *celebrate* yourself. If people don't do it for us, then we need to create that sense of reward for ourselves. And while milestones certainly warrant a reward, we also need to reward ourselves for the small accomplishments we make along the way. For instance, I give myself a reward for going to the gym three times a week. One of my favorites is to reward myself with a thirty minute bike ride on my favorite bicycle path. They don't have to be *big* rewards.

One of the things that has been very helpful to me is to create a *Nurture Myself List*—a list of things you can do to nurture yourself. You could go to a movie you've wanted to see, or try out a new restaurant. For me, it might be going to see Paul McCartney in concert.

Make a *Nurture Myself List* and put it on your bathroom mirror. If you need something to pick you up, reward yourself with something on your list. When I start to feel undeserving and lonely, my creativity starts to diminish. It's like I need a friend to say, "Hey, snap out of it!" My nurturing list is a way to snap myself out of it and remind myself of things I can do to make myself feel good.

Not all of our goals will come in the time frames that we expect, but we must keep working toward them.

One thing that I have maintained over the years is an *Excitement Fund*. Every time I reach a milestone, or reach a small goal, I take a $20 or $100 bill, depending on what I accomplished, and put it in my wallet to carry around with me. I have a predetermined amount that I will *withdraw* from my Excitement Fund once I attain a specific goal. For example, I may have $2000 as my predetermined amount to withdraw for a certain goal. When I reach that goal, I will spend that $2000 on something soley for me. I might take guitar lessons for a year or go to San Francisco for a short fun trip. Make a rule that you can't spend the money on anyone else. You can't even spend it on your children. It has to be for YOU.

The neat effect of the Excitement Fund is that when I start having small or large successes, what does my subconscious want to have more of? *Success*. You need to start giving yourself the experiences of success. You will start having a much more exciting life.

Henry Ford said, "Whether you think you can or whether you think you can't, you're right."

Let's go through a couple of key fundamentals about goals.

Goals have to be meaningful enough to create excitement. Unless you are excited, motivated, and determined about what you are working toward, then a goal is going to be very empty and halt your progress. The goal doesn't have to be something for *you*. Doing things for others is sometimes more compelling than doing things for ourselves. One of the first things Elvis Presley did when he got his first big check, was to buy his mother a pink Cadillac. I'm sure that made him very happy.

Goals need to be long-range because there are going to be some frustrations along the way. There are going to be people who disappoint us. There are going to be activities that, while they are necessary steps toward reaching the goal, are going to be difficult. And there are going to be incidents that discourage us. Keeping our long-range goal in mind will help us through these frustrating times.

There are no unrealistic goals, only unrealistic timelines.

Secondly, **goals need to be specific**, and they need to have a timeline. Many times, when I ask people about their goals, they give me very general statements. "I want more money." "I want a big house." Or, "I want a nice car." Statements like that *won't get it*. You have to be much more specific.

If you want more money, you must write out, "I will have $100,000.00 in my savings account by June 1st 2014." If you want a big house, you must write out, "I will have a 4,000 square foot house in the Nashville, Tennessee area close to Cool Springs Mall, and I will have it by December 1, 2015." For the car you want, you would write out, "I will have a brand new electric Nissan Leaf by January 15, 2012."

As you rewrite these goals every day, you should add "action" as part of the process, such as, "I am very excited to be the first person on my block to be driving the new all electric Nissan Leaf. I love the fact that I am not using gas to power this beautiful new car."

Start with the words "I am." The most powerful words

in the English language are "I am." When you start with the words "I am," your subconscious takes what comes after as a *command*.

The purpose of an affirmation is to evoke a picture, because the *picture* has more power than the words. **The image is more powerful than the thought**. For your affirmations, use action words that end in –ing. If you use active verbs, it propels you with more energy.

Affirmations need to include an adverb. *I am **happily** driving my car. I am **proudly** showing someone my home. I am **peacefully** interacting with my children.* Why do we want an expressive word in there? Your motivation for doing everything is because of how you think it is going to make you *feel* once you have done it. In order to be motivated, we need to use words that stimulate desire.

Thirdly, you need to develop a detailed road map for achieving your goals. You can know *what* you want, *why* you want it, and *who* will help you get there; but the critical ingredient that determines your success is your *actions*. To guide those actions, you must create a step-by-step written plan—a road map.

For a number of years I was a General Contractor and built a number of houses. At the onset, I was somewhat inexperienced, so I approached the building process the way any new, inexperienced builder should. I would get a very detailed blue print that had several pages of drawings, and I would take that blue print to the local lumber dealer. They would put together a detailed cost estimate that included everything we would need to build the house. I bought a book called *Everything You Need to Know to Build a House.* It had step-by-step instructions of what to do from beginning to end. If I had tried to build a house without buying the book, the blue prints, and the complete materials list, I would have been overwhelmed and probably quit half-way through.

Over time, I got to know a few builders. Because they had been building houses so long, they didn't seem to need all the detail and step-by-step instructions that I did, but being a novice, I needed all the help I could get.

This is an example of why so few people ever make any of their dreams come true. They try to build their dream house without the right plans and tools necessary to create it.

It is the same with life. You have to put together your own "blue print" for success. What are the actions you must take consistently to produce the result you desire? If you're not sure, search out someone who has already accomplished what you want to accomplish, and ask them for advice. With so much information on the Internet, all you need to do is type into Google, *What steps do I need to take to become a home builder?* Or your Google search might be, *What steps do I need to take to become a successful singer?*

Be specific. *What steps do I need to take to become a successful* **country** *singer?* Read the autobiography of Reba McEntire. Or watch the movie, *Coal Miner's Daughter*. Those two things will certainly show you the steps—and the long road—to becoming a country singer. There is so much information on the Internet, you can find just about anything on just about any subject that you can dream up.

Another fundamental key to reaching a goal is that you

must take action. It is the discipline of following that plan *no matter what it takes* to reach that goal. You can't just go to work every day, come home, sit in front of the TV, and expect things to happen. Reaching a goal requires studying, planning, and the dedication of finding out what needs to be done today—whatever's next, do it.

You can't *just* visualize and affirm, you have to take action, and if you want to accomplish really great things, you have to take *massive* action. Have you ever known someone who had a lot of really good ideas—they were really bright—but they just couldn't seem to make their life work?

On the flip side, have you ever known someone, or read about someone, who didn't graduate from high school, yet they owned a ton of real estate, or owned one of the larger businesses in town? Just having a formal education doesn't guarantee success. You have to get out there and take action. You have to do something that leads you closer to your dreams.

Take Aristotle Onassis. After his family's wealth was lost in the aftermath of World War I, Aristotle moved to Argentina at the age of seventeen, with sixty bucks in his pocket, and got a job at a telephone company.

Not satisfied just working for the phone company, Aristotle daydreamed about what he wanted to do, until he came up with an idea to start an import-export business. He knew of a wealthy businessman, and he tried to get an appointment with this man to discuss a business idea and potential partnership.

Onassis tried through conventional ways to get an appointment with the wealthy businessman, but he was unable to get past his assistant. After trying for a while, Onassis decided to go stand on the man's doorstep until he could get an appointment.

Committed to his goal, he stayed at this man's doorstep for three weeks and never left. The businessman would come and go to work and see Onassis standing there. Finally, the man asked Onassis what he was doing on his doorstep. Onassis replied that he was trying to get an appointment with him. When the businessman asked Onassis what was so important, he said he would let him know if he would let him walk him to his car.

Between the time they left the building and short distance to the car, Onassis sold the wealthy businessman on his idea, and the two men made a deal. From that day, Onassis worked tirelessly to pursue his dream, and he became one of the richest men that ever lived. What Aristotle Onassis displayed is **perseverance**—simply never giving up.

The average millionaire in America files bankruptcy three times before they "get it right." This means they go big, lose it all, and start over; go big, lose it all and start over; go big, lose it all and start over. Get the picture?

Are you willing to stumble and fall, but then get back up and work some more—*until* you get what you want? You MUST! You *must* be ready to fail and you *must* be resilient. There is rarely any other way. So called "failures" are learning experiences. While resilient people may lose all their money and possessions, the one thing that never get's taken away from them is their knowledge and experience.

One of the basic rules of success is that as you help others prosper, in turn, they will help you prosper. I believe that if you want to be successful, you need to find ways to serve others. This will encourage them to help you be successful in return. However, the *return* may not always come from the person you served. For example, I may serve my brother, and somewhere down the road, someone else may do something for me. It is like a **law of balance**—you can't give something away without getting something else in return somewhere down the line. You may not get it in the time frame you imagine or in the way you imagine; but I have never had an experience where I gave something away without getting something in return. At the very least, I feel the love and fulfillment for having done it. That fulfillment is what makes the difference.

Henry Ford said, "Thinking is the hardest work there is, which is probably the reason so few engage in it."

I want to go a little deeper into *how* and *why* we *set* and *achieve* our goals. This is a different variation of some of the exercises we have already discussed, but this goes into a little more detail and extends the effectiveness.

I would like you to pick out the five most important goals for you to achieve this year. Write them down. We are looking for the things that can generate the passion that will inspire you to use all of your skills. Once you have chosen your five goals, I would like you to write at least a paragraph about *why* you will achieve these five goals.

I want you to sell yourself on the reasons why you need to achieve these goals. Our purpose, or passion, for doing something is a stronger motivator than the goal we are pursuing, so the purpose of this exercise is to crystallize those reasons. ***Reasons* are the**

difference between being interested and being committed.

There are many things in life we *say* we want, but we often end up being interested in them for only a short time. In order for goals to be achieved, we need to be committed to doing whatever it takes to achieve them. If you say to yourself, *I want to be rich,* this statement doesn't tell your brain very much. Why do you want to be rich? Answering the question, *What would being wealthy really mean to me?* That would greatly increase your motivation.

Now make a list of the most important resources you have at your disposal that will assist you in achieving these goals. When I was building houses, I needed to have on hand whatever tools it would take to build that house, such as a hammer and a circular saw. You need to do the same thing with your project—your goal. Make a list of what *resources* you already have, such as character traits, friends, financial resources, education, time, and energy.

Come up with an "inventory" of strengths, tools, and skills to create a resource list that you can pull from in the future. If you think this through very carefully, I'll bet you'll find that you have more resources than you realized. Most of us do.

I would like you to think about three times in your life when you used those skills and resources from your inventory list to achieve a goal. Were these achievements related to business, or sports, or maybe even a relationship? It can be anything from a big sale that you made, to a baseball game where you were at your best, or to a time when you counseled a friend and inspired them. Write down these three achievements and what you did that made them successful. What were the qualities or resources that resulted in success?

Take a moment, close your eyes, and visualize these past experiences. Enhance them by making them bigger, bring them closer to you, and make them more focused. Feel the same feelings that you felt when you were having these experiences. Crystallize these thoughts and emotions so that you can reference them in the future.

Let's use this same exercise to visualize your future. Enlarge the "pictures" of your future. Make them more focused and brighter, and step into your future as if you were there. Visualize yourself acting as if you have already achieved those goals. See the image of this achievement in living color, like a movie. Hear the sounds you would hear and feel the feelings you would feel if you had already achieved these goals. If you do this on a regular basis, you will burn these thoughts and desires into your nervous system. If you learn to use this technique for everything in life, you will be able to create the feeling of success inside of you right now.

Learn to visualize your success as a bright, vivid movie and feel the excitement.

There is a very major key to getting what you want and it's pretty simple—but imperative. A lot of people have trouble with it, they feel they are imposing, or they just don't seem to be able to raise the courage to do it.

The key is simply the practice of **asking**.

How likely is it that you will ever get what you want if you never ask? I have a good friend in Franklin, Kentucky. His name is Ardie Baxter. He is always joking about something he wants from me, and then he follows up by saying, "It never hurts to ask, right?" I swear, I have done more for Ardie than I ever thought I would, just because *he asked*. There have been times that I have thought, *I can't believe you are asking me this*, but then after we talked, I ended up doing what he asked. Asking does take courage, but if you are going to get where you want to go, you are going to have to learn to have lots of courage.

Again, if you don't ask, you will surely never get anything.

I have been in sales for a good share of my life and have attended many sales training seminars. One of the first lessons in being a great sales person is to *never leave without asking for the order*. Tony Robbins says we need to learn to ask intelligently, be very specific about our request, and make sure we are asking the right people. He presents a list of ways he thinks we should "ask" in his book, *Unlimited Power—The New Science of Personal Achievement*, and I recommend reading his list, it has a lot of merit.

Although asking the right people does make sense in a lot of ways, you don't always know who the *right* person may be. There is an old saying, "*Never judge a book by its cover.*" The practice of asking requires this same attitude. You never really know what any person's past experiences have been, who they may know, or what resources they may have.

We should always ask politely, but ask anyone and

everyone for help to get the things in life that we really want.

As Tony Robbins suggests in his list, don't just ask someone for a million dollars, take the money, and never give anything back. That would not only be a foolish request and very self-centered, but it would also leave you empty—as it should. An important technique to keep in mind when asking for something is to keep asking until you reach every goal you have—which will be forever.

The last step is being **grateful**. It's giving thanks to other people and being grateful for what you have right now. Take time to thank all the people who help you get to where you're going.

It was written that one of the ways George W. Bush ascended to Presidency was that he wrote Thank You notes every morning to people that he had worked with, or who had volunteered or helped him in some way. Every morning his assistant would set a stack of Thank You cards on his desk. When he got to his office, the first order of business—before he did anything else—was to *personally* write out and sign Thank You notes to his *list* for the day.

A few years ago I made this same commitment. I make sure to take the time to thank people for what they do for me. This is one of the reasons I came up with the Gratitude Coin. I wanted a very memorable way of saying *thank you* to people for their help, their kindness, or their smile. Think about this practice and consider making it a part of your daily routine. It will pay for itself many times over.

Take a few minutes and make a list of the activities, the

resources, and the people in your life that you are most grateful for. This list is great to look at whenever you are feeling less resourceful. It will boost your frame of mind. We all have to admit that we have been guilty of taking what we have for granted. It's easy to get so fixated on what we hope to have next year that we forget to appreciate or use what we already have. A good first step in moving forward is recognizing what you have and being thankful for it.

I believe that True Wealth is built on a foundation of gratitude.

Zig Ziglar tells a story of a young sailor at sea. The sailor was on a ship that had run into a big storm. The captain ordered him to climb the mast to fix one of the sails. As the sailor climbed up the mast, a swell came up, and he made the mistake of looking down. He could see the swells of the ocean and the frightening turbulence of the sea. He lost his balance and was about to slip. The captain yelled, "Look up!" The young man immediately looked up, caught his balance, and steadied himself.

The moral of this story is that *when life starts to look bad—and that will happen, make certain you are not looking in the wrong direction*. When you take your eyes off the goal, then you focus on the problems. If you want to reach your goals, then you must keep your eyes on your goals. **Remember to focus on what you want, not on what you don't want.**

Mark Twain once said, "I am an old man and have

known a great many troubles, but most of them never happened!"

Results are inevitable. If you don't *program* your mind with desired results, someone else will provide the *programming* for you. If you don't have your own plan for your life, someone else will make you fit into their plan.

It is imperative that you do each of the exercises that I have laid out. They may not be easy at first, but they are worth every ounce of "sweat," and as you do them, they will become more and more fun.

One of the reasons more people don't do as well in life is because success often requires a lot of hard work. Goal setting and success don't come overnight. We have become addicted to TV and movies where someone's whole life passes before us in thirty minutes, or at most, a couple of hours. It has created a false sense of reality in our expectations for expediency and has caused emotional complacency.

And there are those who are so afraid of success that they hide behind needing to "get a few more projects done" before they get started. It is so easy for people to put off hard work like this, as they get caught up in making a living, instead of spending a few hours a week designing their lives.

It has been said that there are only two pains in life. One is the pain of discipline, and the other the pain of regret. Discipline weighs ounces, while regret weighs tons.

Remember, you now have the tools to make your life better at any moment.

Achieving your wildest dreams begins today.

Self-Confidence in Action

Self-confidence *in action* is seen a number of different ways. It means accepting complete responsibility for yourself. If you believe that anyone else is responsible for how you act or respond to life, then you are using that as a crutch to allow yourself the "out", *It is someone else's fault that I am who I am*. This is not to say that you haven't been influenced by a host of events—and people—that have helped to establish the habit patterns and self-talk that have become part of your life to this point. But—from this day forward—they cannot be your crutch, because you now know that you *can* and *will* change for the better.

Always do more than you are asked to do and contribute more than is required. I believe doing more than what is expected of me, and more than what another person would do, puts me in a position of power. If I have exceeded my performance expectations, I feel that *I* can be in control of my day more than others. If everyone in your department works from nine to five, but you work until six, then you will stand out as a hard worker and be appreciated by your employer.

If I am a sales person who works that extra hour every night to finish my paperwork and there comes a time when I need to take some time to handle a personal matter, I know my employer will gladly comply.

There are plenty of people who would take that time during work hours, whether they had earned the time off or not, but those people will die broke while complaining that "life isn't fair." And from this day forward, that will never be you. Your "savings account" in life will always have plenty.

Anytime you start a new project and you are assessing your strategy,ask yourself, *What is the biggest factor that would limit my ability to accomplish this goal?* Your ability to identify that *factor* is one of the most valuable skills you can learn. For many people, their greatest limiting factor is their level of self-confidence. If you have enough self-confidence, you can learn almost anything and overcome most any obstacle.

Any time someone overcomes an obstacle, it is because they "figured it out." Through trial and error, they learned how to avoid or work through that obstacle. When you have enough self-confidence, there is virtually nothing you won't try—no obstacle you cannot overcome. **Because successes are largely a matter of the law of averages, the more things you try, the more you will achieve.**

When you win that *inner* battle, the *outer* battles are

surmountable, and you overcome them. The development of greater self-confidence enables one to go from rags to riches, from limited means to unlimited resources. Talent and ambition are critical but those are qualities and skills you can learn once you have developed unstoppable self-confidence.

Every successful man or woman I have ever talked to has the same opinion. Everyone can garner more talent and ability than they can ever use—with the right mindset. You must develop the self-confidence to step on the "accelerator" of your own potential. When you do you will move forward at a speed that will amaze you.

Incorporating the following four skills and emotions into your nervous system will give you unstoppable self-confidence.

Desire: The intensity of your desire to have immense self-confidence must be so strong that it overrides your fears of failure, rejection, and inferiority, and becomes the dominant emotion influencing your actions.

Decisiveness: You must make a "do or die" decision and keep at it until you achieve the kind of self-confidence that allows you to do and be whatever you want.

Determination: Your determination must be as unshakable as the self-confidence you desire. Sometimes progress will seem so slow that you will feel like you have come to the end of the line, and others will tell you there is no hope. Because you are committed to your goals, you know you *must* persist. You have faith in yourself, and you know that your determination will lead to you becoming the person you wish to be.

Discipline: The foundation of all great achievement is the quality of self-discipline. The ability to make yourself do *what* you should do *when* you should do it, whether you feel like it or not. If you have the desire to change, the decisiveness to take action, the determination to persist, and the discipline to make yourself do whatever you need to do, your self-confidence—and ultimately your success—is inevitable.

Every success you experience builds your self-esteem and improves your ability to achieve more success. As you achieve small successes, you will gain the confidence to try new challenges. Every mental exercise that you engage in to improve your character, improves your confidence. Everything that you learn and practice from this book, all the skills you learn from watching the lives of other self-confident people, will improve your own self-confidence and self-esteem.

In the mid 1980s, the Gallup organization developed one of the most exhaustive surveys into the reasons for success ever conducted in America. They selected fifteen hundred men and women whose names and bios appeared in the *Who's Who in America*. They inquired of them, at great length, what they felt was the reason they were so well-known in their lifetime.

The group included Nobel Prize winners, university professors, heads of corporations, writers, etc., and even a high school football coach. After many months of research and interviews, the surveyors were able to isolate the five most important qualities for success and self-confidence in America. The first and most important quality of all was **common sense**. The participants defined common sense as the ability to "cut to the core" of the matter. They had learned to recognize and deal with the essential elements of a problem or a situation, rather than get sidetracked by lesser issues or symptoms.

Common sense was the ability to learn from past experiences and apply those lessons to fresh experiences. Perhaps another word for common sense is wisdom. The Greek philosopher, Aristotle, once wrote, "Wisdom is an equal combination of experience plus reflection." Most people are far wiser than they give themselves credit for. It is their lack of self-confidence that stops them from using their common sense.

The two best questions that will spark personal growth are: *What did I do right? ...and...What would I do differently?* After every experience, successful or not, stop and visualize an instant replay of the experience and ask yourself these two questions. Take a piece of paper and write at the top of the page, *What did I do right?* By analyzing your immediate performance, you will be accelerating your development of common sense. That you take the time to reflect will alone improve your skills.

When you ask, *What would I do differently?* you see all kinds of possibilities for improvement. The wonderful thing about these two questions is that the answer to both is positive and constructive. When you dwell on the positive, constructive parts of your performance—both present and future—these parts sink deeper in to your subconscious and program you to act consistentlye with that information the next time out.

The second quality the *Who's Who* had in common was **expertise**. Super successful men and women excel at what they do, and they *know* it. They have learned, practiced, and grown until they are recognized by their peers as the "cream of the crop". This feeling of being the best is an absolute prerequisite for deep and lasting self-confidence.

The third quality the *Who's Who* shared was **self-reliance**. Men and women who are respected by others look primarily to themselves for the solutions to their problems. They are highly responsible individuals, and they don't blame others when things go wrong. Their will alone is the primary force for accomplishment. They volunteer for tough assignments and are willing to take charge when a leader is needed.

The fourth common quality of the *Who's Who* was that of **intelligence** or **street smarts**. There is no question that intelligence is a key factor for success in any field, but when the surveyors considered "intelligence," they didn't measure it in terms of IQ. Many of the most successful men and women had not done that well in school and many had not completed high school or college.

Once in the business world, you must take the time and effort to educate yourself to be very knowledgeable (intelligent) in your field—that's part of your commitment to your success. Whenever you do something that moves you forward toward achieving your goals, you are behaving intelligently. Whenever you engage in behavior that moves you away from your goals, you are behaving foolishly. The world is full of people who behave foolishly, but that won't be you. You have chosen to behave differently.

If you are in sales and you manage your time well, that is acting intelligently. If you have a big sales presentation to do on Friday, but on Wednesday you go to a ballgame instead of working and preparing, you are acting inconsistently with your goals. Here is the key: everything you do is either moving you toward your goals or away from your goals. Nothing is neutral. Each act you engage in is either positive or it is negative.

The fifth shared quality of the *Who's Who* was a **result-orientation**. This means that *you* take the responsibility of accomplishing whatever task you pursue. All high achievers are those who can get the job done, whatever it is. They are "action" people who are results-focused. They take action with a sense of urgency, a vital skill that must be acquired and ultimately determines your success. You will be promoted rapidly and more often. You will be offered more money because you will be producing a higher quantity and quality of work.

You will undoubtedly receive other job offers. And you will be immune to economic downturns, because your services will be invaluable. By developing intense results-orientation, you guarantee yourself success.

Here are a few thoughts about self-confidence in action. First, I want to revisit a point I made earlier about buying some nice clothes to "dress yourself up." I rarely buy designer clothes, unless I get them on sale at a store like Nordstrom Rack. However, I do purchase quality clothing. I wear plain white shirts made by Lands End. They are great quality, but are not an expensive designer brand, so they cost a third or less than a popular designer shirt. I don't have a passion to wear designer clothing, because I feel that the cost is way out of line. It's easy to see why Ralph Lauren and Tommy Hilfiger are billionaires just from using their names to sell clothing and accessories.

Our culture *decides* our status based on what we wear and drive, rather than *knowing* who we are by our thoughts and actions. As your self-image grows, it will lessen your need to wear designer clothing, drive the brand of car you think you *should*, or make someone else rich while you live paycheck to paycheck, just so you can have the outward appearance of being successful.

It is more rewarding to build your savings account up, rather than spending it on showy items. The larger your savings account, the more self-confidence you will have, knowing that you have cash to weather an unexpected financial crisis. It is amazing what having a nice, healthy cash reserve will do for your self-confidence.

For years I have been running around the country speaking to audiences about making money and becoming financially independent. It is my belief that—for most people—if you really want to become financially independent, the foundation stone is learning to live below your means. This is so profound that I have to say it again**. If you really want to become financially independent, the foundation stone is learning to live below your means.**

This does not mean that you need to live like a pauper, as that existence will never give you the passion to keep working. It just means, that if you make $500 a week, you need to live on $450 and save the rest. If you make $10,000 a week, then live on roughly $5,000 a week and save the other $5,000. How much to live on and how much to save are amounts you will have to decide for yourself. You will have to find out what works for you—but you will never be financially independent, if you don't learn to live within your means.

We have become attached to outside hollow, appearances rather than focusing on our works and accomplishments for validation. As your mindset changes about your self-esteem, so will your mindset change about *you*. Your need for designer clothing, cars, or whatever external splurges tempt you, will change.

Having said that, if buying a couple of Ralph Lauren outfits is the *dramatic* step that gets you started, then I'm all for it. If it serves a purpose in starting you on the path of feeling worthy as you build a healthy self-image, it is worth it. Just don't make a habit of it.

One of the dreams that I had from a fairly young age was to have a Rolex watch. I thought they were beautiful, and at the time, I was convinced that having a stainless and gold Rolex watch would tell the world that I had made it.

I thought it would make me feel good to achieve the goal of owning a Rolex, so when I was about twenty-seven years old, I made the decision to get one. I went to a jewelry store and the gentleman that waited on me said, "This Rolex is a beautiful watch, and it's a good, quality watch that will last a long time. However, unless you *need* a Rolex, I would recommend another brand, because the Rolex is not that great at keeping time."

He claimed that the newer brands had better technology for about the same price—or maybe even a little less. He recommended a few other brands that were very stylish and better at keeping time. However, he *did* also say that if I was looking for a watch for my self-esteem, and "the Rolex really *does it* for you, then maybe the Rolex is the watch for you." I said, "A Rolex has been a long-term dream, and it's the watch I want." He said, "Okay, I have them in stock, but I am going to discount it, so that I don't feel bad that I sold it to you."

I bought the watch, and I have had it for thirty years. It really did make me feel good for a long time; but today, I don't need the Rolex to make me feel good, and I would not have one, if I didn't already have the one I bought. The watch did serve a purpose for me for a while. It was one of those dramatic things that I did which gave me the feeling of accomplishment. It is okay to do nice things for yourself and those around you—if you have the means to do it.

Here is a story that reveals supreme self-confidence. I read this story years ago, but was so inspired by the message it conveyed, that I have kept it close for years.

A New York businessman's company had gotten into serious trouble. He had lost some of his biggest customers and was deeply in debt to his suppliers and creditors. Feeling the walls closing in on him, he wasn't sure whether he should continue to struggle or declare bankruptcy and go out of business.

In an effort to clear his head he went for a walk in the park one evening. He was standing on a bridge overlooking the park when an old man appeared. Seeing the businessman's downcast look, the older gentleman stopped and asked, "What's the matter?" Feeling depressed and in need of someone to talk to, he told the older gentleman all about his financial problems. He told him how close his business was to collapsing, even though he knew the company had a lot of potential. The older gentleman listened, and then said, "I think I can help you."

He pulled out his checkbook, asked the businessman his name, and proceeded to write out a check. He then folded the check and put it in the businessman's hand and said, "Take this money. Meet me here exactly one year from today, and you can pay me back at that time." Then the older gentleman turned and disappeared into the darkness.

When the businessman went back to his office, he opened up the check and found out that it was for $500,000.00. The signature read, John D. Rockefeller. He had received a check for half a million dollars from the richest man in the world at that time, the man that had formed the Standard Oil Company and was well-known for giving money to others.

At first the businessman thought he would cash the check and solve all his financial problems. But then he decided that he would put the check in his safe, knowing that he could draw upon it any time. He would use the knowledge of having the money to help him deal more confidently with his suppliers and creditors and turn his business around.

So with renewed enthusiasm, he plunged back into his business, made deals, negotiated settlements, extended payment terms, and closed several large sales. Within a few months, his business was out of debt, back on top, and making money.

One year later, he went back to the bridge with the still uncashed check in his hand. He could hardly wait to tell the old gentleman what had happened. At exactly the agreed upon time, the older gentleman emerged from the darkness once more. Just as the businessman was about to give him back the check, tell him about his business, and how much success he had achieved over the last year, a nurse came running out of the darkness and grabbed the older man by his arm. She apologized to the businessman, saying, "I am so glad I caught him. I hope he hasn't been bothering you. He is always escaping from the rest-home and going around telling people that he is John D. Rockefeller." She took the older gentleman's arm and led him away.

The businessman stood there stunned. All year long he had been wheeling and dealing, buying and selling, building his business with the calm, confident knowledge that he had a $500,000.00 check in his safe that he could cash at anytime. As the event raced through is mind, it dawned on him that he had made his business a success based on his *beliefs*. Even though he had been holding a $500,000.00 check that wasn't good, it had been his self-confidence in action that was responsible for his success over the past year.

Your job now is to achieve the same level of self-confidence and belief possessed by that businessman. The world doesn't know what your situation is, and in most cases they accept what you present. It is *you* that needs to be convinced before anyone else.

There are many stories that tell of overcoming incredible odds and doing things that are unbelievable. A short time ago, I read an article that told the incredible story of someone doing more than what seemed humanly possible—yet they did.

> *June 23, 2011, Yahoo News-Amazing Tales: USF lineman lifts Cadillac, saves trapped man by Matt Hinton—*
>
> *Danous Estenor may sound like the name of a character from a Tolkien novel, and he may look like a grizzly bear that could maul anyone who crosses his path. At 6-foot-3, 306 pounds, he probably could, actually. Off the field, though, the South Florida*

offensive lineman is more of the gentle giant type, more likely to channel his natural power to more productive ends — such as last February, for example, when he hulked out on a 3,500-pound car to save a man trapped underneath.

From Friday's St. Petersburg Times:

Across the parking lot on that Thursday night in February, [Estenor] saw a frightening scene: a tow truck driver pinned under the rear tire of a 1990 Cadillac Seville that had lurched forward as he worked underneath it, his wife struggling in vain with two men to lift the car.

"I just see his legs," said Estenor, 21, a child of Haitian immigrants from Palm Beach. "The car is crushing him. He's not moving. I'm thinking, Oh, God, this guy is going to die."

"I tried to lift the car, and when I first tried, it didn't budge. I backed up. I don't know. But I felt this energy come, and I lifted it. I don't know how, but somebody pulled him from under the car." Maria Uribe had been sleeping in the cab of her husband's truck when she heard Arzola, 34, yelling, "Help me."

The scene looked "Like a horror movie ... a lot of blood," she said. The Cadillac's front right tire had run over Arzola's torso and dragged him about 10 feet. Somehow he sustained only cuts, bruises, and a dislocated shoulder, which was pinned beneath the rear tire. He was back towing cars two weeks later.

Estenor's immediate response to the incident was to continue on to the cafeteria for dinner.

Even teammates were skeptical of his adrenaline-fueled heroism, until a few weeks later, when Coach Skip Holtz brought Estenor in front of the team, while he read a letter from the manager of the Bull's Den Cafe, in whose parking lot the accident occurred. Two Bull's Den employees, including the owner of the Cadillac, were attempting (unsuccessfully) to lift the car when Estenor came to the rescue. "Ever since coach Holtz read the letter, they all say, 'Oh, where's your cape?'" he told the Times. "It's not bad. They're just making fun, but I'm glad Holtz let them know what happened. I always feel good when I do a good deed, to help somebody, any kind of way."

Yes, the heart is warmed. Now how does Estenor recreate the same adrenaline rush when handling defensive linemen?

What a great story of someone doing something they never would have believed they could do, but they did. Again, we are all capable of more than we think we are.

Every time you commit to going the extra mile, put in more than you take out, and go beyond what is expected of you in your job and in your relationships, you will feel terrific about yourself. Your level of self-confidence increases and you feel motivated to give more of yourself in every endeavor. When you dedicate yourself to excellence, you feel an enhanced sense of mastery and competence.

Create a positive and suggestive environment around yourself, and create clear mental pictures of who you want to be and things you want to accomplish. Read books that expand your mind and increase your abilities. Before you fall asleep, think about the things you did *right* during the day and focus on those accomplishments.

Get away from negativity. Soak your mind in positive images of you at your best. Whenever something happens that throws you off balance, stabilize yourself by thinking about your goals. When you think about your goals, your mind will instantly become positive again. This is an example of the **law of substitution**—you can only think one thought at a time.

Whenever you have the choice of doing something easy but meaningless versus something hard but necessary, force yourself out of your comfort zone and toward your dreams. Resist the temptation to go easy on yourself. **Remember, the comfort zone is the enemy to great performance and potential.**

The more you dare to go forward, the more likely this type of courageous behavior will become a habit for you. You will gradually "act" yourself into feeling fearless in almost any situation, and there won't be anything you won't attempt. You will develop such confidence that your belief in your ability to succeed, even against incredible odds, will be rock-solid.

Perhaps your greatest responsibility to yourself is to **become a person of action**. Your primary job is to make every effort to overcome any obstacle and become the unstoppable, self-confident person you are capable of becoming. Once you achieve unshakable self-confidence, everything is possible.

Perseverance

Perseverance is working toward your goals, no matter what arises to discourage you. Perseverance is going that last mile, even though you are so tired that you have a hard time keeping your head up—but you do, and you make it. Perseverance is forging on, *even* when your friends and family tell you there is no chance you will make it—but *you* know you can, and you do.

One of the most basic traits common to successful individuals, is that they all have a profound belief in themselves. With this faith and the focus and commitment to their goals, they radiate their will to the universe and it complies.

They have been able to bend and grow with the winds of change, without breaking their spirit. This ability to bend and spring back is demonstrated in their unusual adaptability to whatever comes up.

They look at the bright side of the darkest situations. They have the determination—the perseverance—to make themselves do the things that others are not willing to do. I didn't say *not able to do*, I said *not willing to do*.

I have heard people say they are *putting their faith in a miracle.* But haven't most miracles been proven to be faith or perseverance in action? When someone says, "What has happened is a miracle," what is said in the next breath is, "Our prayers were answered. We never gave up hope that if we just kept on working, we could see it through." Maybe an undeniable belief in you *IS* the miracle.

Maybe that is why real success is such a well-kept secret. Everyone wants it. Most people spend countless days and years dreaming of it. Everyone talks and writes about it, or goes to meetings to hear more about it. But that is as far as it goes. Why is it that so few achieve it?

The dramatic change in economic attitude throughout the world has brought so much prosperity to so many countries, and with that change, so much more opportunity. It is not the same world as it was even twenty years ago. We have seen so much change from Russia, to India, and to Asia; with China fast-becoming the richest nation in the world.

I can't imagine what opportunities will open up as we see the Middle East and Africa develop; as the dictators continue to be overthrown, and those countries are allowed to grow and prosper.

I am so excited for the development of the Middle East and Africa, as the people launch new business ventures in their countries and do what the people of the United States have been allowed to do for more than two hundred years. It really feels as if their time has come to prosper—a time that is long overdue.

In the United States, we have had such an economic mess in the last few years that the majority of people are unsure and depressed about what opportunity might be left in our country. We still throw out more garbage every week than most people in underdeveloped countries eat in a year. One Thanksgiving dinner for an American family of five would feed twenty starving people in one of the underdeveloped nations for a month. No economic condition in this country could even begin to match the conditions that exist in some areas of the world.

Mr. T, of the *Rocky III* movie and *The A-Team* TV series echos a sentiment that I know well, "I was born and raised in the ghetto, but the ghetto was not born and raised in me." It is all too easy to use the way you were raised, or a variety of other excuses, for not doing more with your life, but if Mr. T can overcome his beginnings, then so can you.

Yes, there is poverty, discrimination, bigotry, ignorance, and injustice in this world; but, if you remain open, you can find more information, opportunity and openness, than ever before in the history of the world. Show me someone who has succeeded in the face of incredible odds, and I will show you a person who knows what perseverance entails.

There are so many stories where people have overcome incredible odds. The deck was stacked so far out of their favor that you wonder how they ever overcame those obstacles, but they did. I have always thought this kind of "triumph over the odds" story builds such incredible emotion and keeps your intensity so high, that you keep moving forward and always hold your head high. I would like to share a couple of these stories with you to continue building your mindset of perseverance and determination.

ASU's 2011 Valedictorian is Undocumented

This story appeared as a Spotlight on the *Phoenix New Times* blogs page on May 12, 2011.

Angelica Hernandez has been in America since the age of 9. In 1998, her mother brought Angelica and her sister across the border with the plan of reuniting them with their father, who was already working in Phoenix, Arizona. When they arrived in the U.S., Angelica's mother discovered that the girls' father had been having an affair. Despite the heartbreak, the mother decided to stay in America, in the hopes of building a better life than they had in Zacatecas. Angelica's mother did not speak English. She didn't have a green card to be able to go get a "regular" job. She worked at whatever jobs she could get, but they struggled to make ends meet. In America, unlike Mexico, school is available to all children, no matter their circumstances (citizenship). Because of this, Angelica's mother was able to enroll both her daughters in the local school. She told her daughters that if they worked hard and did their best, they would have a better life.

Angelica did work hard over the next several years. She excelled in school, graduating from high school with a 4.5 GPA ,and earning a name for herself in

> *the school's famed robotics program. She received a scholarship and was accepted to ASU's Engineering Program. After 4 more years of hard work , Angelica Hernandez graduates as a Valedictorian of Arizona State University class of 2011.*

What an accomplishment!

From walking from Zacatecas, Mexico, to Phoenix in 1998; to being raised by a non-English speaking single mother of two; to Valedictorian of ASU. If that isn't a story of perseverance, I don't know what is!

Piers Morgan, of CNN's *Piers Morgan Tonight,* recently interviewed comedian Tom Arnold. Arnold talked about being raised in a small farming town in Iowa. His parents divorced when he was about four, and his mother had major issues with alcohol, remarrying seven times as Tom grew up. Tom said that he had been sexually abused by a male baby-sitter during this time, and he felt devastated by it throughout his childhood.

On another episode of his show, Piers Morgan interviewed comedian George Lopez. Lopez grew up in the inner city of Los Angeles, never knowing his father. His mother also had major issues with alcohol. She left George with his grandmother to raise him. Lopez said his grandmother didn't have much for parenting skills either, so he grew up getting into trouble all the time.

Both Tom Arnold and George Lopez have climbed to the top of the ladder in their fields despite major obstacles that would have keep most people down. It's *not what* circumstances you were dealt in life, but *what you do* with those circumstances that determines where life will take you.

Years ago I read the story of Wilma Rudolph. It is such an inspiring story that it still moves me to tears.

Born prematurely June 23, 1940, weighing only 4.5 pounds, Wilma Rudolph had complications that resulted in her contracting double pneumonia twice as well as scarlet fever. Wilma did not get what you would call a head start in life.

At a young age Wilma contracted infantile paralysis (caused by the polio virus) that left her with a twisted leg and unable to walk correctly. She had to wear leg braces and go through treatments at a hospital in Nashville that was a 45-mile bus ride south of her small town, Clarksville, Tennessee.

Her first vivid thought as a six year-old was, "I am going to travel out of this small town and make my place in the world." She recalls riding the bus to Nashville for her treatments, which went on for six years. While at the hospital, she would always ask the doctor, "When will I get to take off these braces and walk without them?"

Careful not to raise false hopes, he said, "We'll see."

By age eleven, she knew that she would take them off someday. The doctor wasn't so sure, but he did suggest that Wilma's legs should be exercised a little. Wilma decided that a lot of exercise would be better than a little exercise. When her parents would leave the house, one of her brothers or sisters would keep a watch at the door for their return. She would take the braces off every day and painfully walk around the house for hours. If anyone would come in, the "lookout" would help her back on the bed and go through the motions of massaging her legs to justify the braces being off.

This continued for about a year, and though her confidence was growing, so was a gnawing feeling of guilt inside of her. She wondered how to tell her mother of this unauthorized, "do it yourself," rehabilitation program. During her next routine visit to Nashville, Wilma told the doctor, "I have something I would like to share with you."

She proceeded to take the braces off and walked across the office to where he was sitting. She could feel her mother's eyes behind her as she walked, knowing that the actions that brought her to this miraculous moment were strictly against her mother's rules.

"How long have you been doing this?" the doctor questioned, trying to control his surprise.

"About a year," she said, trying not to look directly at her mother. "I sometimes take the braces off and walk around the house."

*"Well, since you have been honest in sharing this with me," he replied, "**Sometimes** I will allow you to take them off and walk around the house." Sometimes was the only permission she needed. She never put them on again. As Wilma turned twelve, she discovered that girls run and jump and play, just like boys. She had been housebound most of her life until then, but had decided— not anymore. As she began to explore her new expanded horizon, she decided to conquer anything that had to do with girls' athletics.*

One of her sisters, Yvonne, was two years older and was trying out for the girls' basketball team, so Wilma decided she should try out also. She was crushed to learn that out of the thirty girls trying out, she wasn't even one of the twelve finalists. She ran home, vowing to show the kids who had played with her that she was good enough.

When Wilma arrived home, she noticed the coach's car in the driveway.

"Oh no!" she thought, "He won't even let me break the news to my own parents."

She went around to the back door and stepped in quietly. She pressed her ear against the door to hear the conversation in the living room. The coach was busy explaining what time Wilma's sister would be home from practice, how many road trips she would take, who would chaperone, and all the details that parents need to know when their daughter makes the team. Her father was not a man of many words, but when he spoke, you knew it was the law.

"There is only one stipulation of Yvonne joining your team," he said.

"Anything you want," assured the coach.

"My girls always travel in two's," he said slowly, "and if you want Yvonne, you will have to take Wilma along to chaperone."

Well, it wasn't exactly what Wilma had in mind, but it was a start. Wilma soon found out that being ***placed*** *on a team by your father, and being* ***selected*** *for the team by the coach, are two entirely different things.*

She could feel the resentment of the twelve other girls, but she also was exhilarated when she saw the uniforms. They were new black satin uniforms. "There is something about your first uniform," she said. "It creates kind of a special feeling of identity." They ran out of uniforms by the time they got to Wilma, so they gave her a green and gold one from the previous year.

"Never mind," she thought, as she sat on the end of the bench through the season. "I'll get my chance."

She finally got the nerve to confront her coach. The 6 foot, 89 pound straggler came into his office and found him.

The coach was a little gruff and very direct as he asked, "Well, what do you want?"

She forgot her prepared speech as she shifted her weight from one foot to the other.

"Speak up," he said. "People who have important things to say get them said. If you don't state what it is, I will never know what your problem is."

She finally blurted out, "If you give me ten minutes of your time, and only ten minutes every day, I will give you in return a world class athlete."

He laughed uncontrollably and could not be certain of the audacity of her words. She turned to leave and he stopped her.

"Wait a minute. I will give you the ten minutes you want, but remember, I am going to be busy with real world class athletes; people who will be getting scholarships and going off to college."

She was so excited, that she wore her uniform to school every day under her street clothes. When the bell would ring, she was the first kid in the gym to receive her precious gift of ten minutes of personal instruction. It became obvious right away that most of the instruction was to be verbal, and that she was making little progress translating the words into basketball skills.

As she sat crying, two boys whom she had known for a long time came up to her and tried to console her. "I really can't understand why it is so hard for me to do what he tells me. I need help," she said softly.

"We will go with you to the ten-minute session, and then we will help show you what the coach is trying to teach you," they volunteered. The next day, they began. Wilma's best girlfriend joined in, and they played two-on-two half-court basketball. Day after day they would listen and practice, mastering the game of basketball.

She became a basketball star at Burt High School and set many state records, leading her team to the state championships. During the state basketball tournament, Ed Temple, the internationally-known track coach of the prestigious Tigerbells of Tennessee State University, spotted her. Under his tutoring, some of the Tigerbells had developed into the fastest women in the country.

Temple invited Wilma to participate in a summer sports camp because Burt High School didn't have a track team. The first time Wilma ran a race, she found she beat her girlfriend. Then she beat all the other girls in her high school, and then every high school girl in the state of Tennessee.

She joined the Tigerbells track team at fourteen, and went into serious training at Tennessee State University. By the end of the summer, she had won the 75-yard and 100-yard dashes and was on the winning 440-yard relay team in the junior division at the national AAU meet in Philadelphia Wilma was eliminated in the semi-finals of the 200-meter dash at the 1956 Olympic games in Melbourne, Australia, but went on to win 3rd place, a bronze medal, as a member of the team in the women's 400-meter relay.

She was partly happy and partly heartbroken for the remainder of her stay in Australia She told herself that this kind of performance wouldn't happen again—that next time, she would get it right. She was only 16, had already won a bronze metal, and was committing herself to win even bigger in the 1960 Olympics.

When we speak of dedication and persistence, we have a tendency to remember only the highlights and to gloss over the agonizing details of what it takes to be a world class anything. One thing to remember about being an athlete back then is that there weren't athletic scholarships for women in those days. Wilma was paying her way as she attended Tennessee State University. At the same time she was going to track workouts every day, it was mandatory for each young woman to maintain a B average and carry eighteen units in order to remain a member of the Tigerbells track team. To give herself the winner's edge, she resorted to a type of extra-curricular do-it-yourself program, similar to what she had used years before when she was learning to walk without leg braces.

When she realized she was slipping behind the other girls on the team because of her work and study load, Wilma began sneaking down the dormitory fire escape to run the track from 8-10 pm, then she would climb back up and head into bed in time for lights out and bed check. At sunrise, the grueling training schedule continued. She would run at 6 am and 10 am, then in the afternoon at 3 pm. Week after week, year after year, she maintained the same monotonous, demanding schedule.

When Wilma walked out on the stadium field in the summer of 1960 in Rome to warm up for the first event, she was ready. "Wilma, Wilma, Wilma," the crowd roared. Eighty-thousand fans began to cheer wildly, sensing that she was to be one of the special Olympians throughout history who would capture the hearts of the spectators.

There was never a doubt in her mind, or in theirs, who was to be standing on the top platform when the award presentations were to be made. She turned in three electrifying performances, breezing to easy victory in the 100-meter and 200-meter dashes and anchoring the U.S. Women's team to a first place finish in the 400-meter relay. Three gold medals. Wilma was the fastest woman in history to ever win three gold medals in track and field. Each of the three races she won was done so in world record time.

Wilma had been a crippled little girl who rode the bus to Nashville, isolated from her neighbors, but supported by her parents, family, and a few loyal friends. Now she was Wilma Rudolph, the Legend.

Wilma finished college and went back to teach and be the track coach at the high school she had attended. For years, Wilma gave speeches or helped some future Olympic star. She also became a Goodwill Ambassador to West Africa. What she said she loved best was giving classes, seminars, and financial support to the Wilma Rudolph Foundation—helping someone get ahead who was coming from behind. Wilma died of brain cancer in 1994. Her autobiography was published in 1977, and I highly recommend it.

Wilma Rudolph turned out to be a winner against incredible odds. She would never let herself be defeated. She set her mind on winning, and she did.

Perhaps Wilma inspired another notable graduate from Tennessee State University, Oprah Winfrey—one more person who certainly knew how to persevere.

Everyone says they want success, but few are willing to pay the price and do the work that is necessary to have it. Zig Ziglar says, "You do not *pay* the price of success, you *enjoy* the price of success."

You know, thinking you can, is only the first step. It takes weeks, months, and years of persistence to overcome the odds. It means doing the tough things and waiting for gratification and rewards. It means being happy with today, but hungry for more knowledge and progress. It means making more sales calls, going more miles, pulling more weeds, getting up earlier in the day, and always being on the lookout for more ways to grow.

Perseverance is learned best through trial and error. There is excitement in knowing that individuals don't reach their prime productivity until much later in life, usually after age forty. For young people, that means there is time to gain knowledge and develop a track record. For us older folks, it means there is still hope.

If Colonel Sanders can build one of the biggest fast food chains in the world starting at age sixty-five; if Angelica Hernandez can walk from Zacatecas, Mexico, with next to nothing, to Phoenix, Arizona, and become a Valedictorian at ASU; if George Lopez and Tom Arnold can overcome their bleak backgrounds and end up wealthy Hollywood stars; and, if a young girl from Tennessee can take off her leg braces and sprint to three gold medals as the fastest woman in the world; then you certainly can make your dreams come true. The secret is perseverance. So, press on, and never give up.

Among the great visionaries of the world, there is a common consensus as to what it means to be successful. As we work toward our dreams, we need to find happiness in the journey that is our day-to-day life, rather than focus on the fantasy of that moment when we are recognized for having arrived.

Although no one will ever achieve total success, and no one is perfect, we all make mistakes. Following your dreams and passions is a definition of success that you can take with you on your journey through life:

Success is the continuing pursuit of a worthy ideal, which is being realized for the benefit of others, rather than at their expense. Success is the process of sharing, learning and growing. Success is having a smile and being happy every day.

There are two great tragedies in life. One is not having a great dream to strive for, and the other is never reaching for and achieving a dream you *do* envision. My life's purpose from this day forward is to empower people and help them find excitement, joy, and fulfillment.

Believe in yourself with passion. Go out and embrace the things in life that really make you happy. And remember that true happiness comes from within.

Be happy, be healthy, be content, be empowered, and go out with that radiant smile and shine to the world, because now you've found true wealth.

To receive a free gratitude coin, please visit our website at www.truewealthuniversity.com.